THE LIFE HISTORY OF THE UNITED STATES

Volume 10: 1917-1932

WAR, BOOM AND BUST

BOOKS

THE LIFE HISTORY OF THE UNITED STATES

THE **LIFE** HISTORY OF THE UNITED STATES

Consulting Editor, Henry F. Graff

Volume 10: 1917-1932

WAR, BOOM AND BUST

by Ernest R. May

and the Editors of LIFE

TIME INCORPORATED, NEW YORK

THE AUTHOR of Volumes 9 and 10 of this series, Ernest R. May, has concentrated on the study of 19th and 20th Century American foreign policy. A professor of history at Harvard University, he has received grants from the Guggenheim Foundation and the Social Science Research Council. During 1963-1964 Professor May was a Fellow at the Center for Advanced Study in the Behavioral Sciences, Stanford, California. He is the author of *Imperial Democracy: The Emergence of America as a Great Power* and *The World War and American Isolation, 1914-1917,* and is editor of *The Ultimate Decision: The President as Commander in Chief.*

THE CONSULTING EDITOR for this series, Henry F. Graff, is Chairman of the Department of History at Columbia University.

TIME-LIFE BOOKS

EDITOR *Norman P. Ross*

TEXT DIRECTOR *William Jay Gold*   ART DIRECTOR *Edward A. Hamilton*

CHIEF OF RESEARCH *Beatrice T. Dobie*

Editorial staff for Volume 10, THE LIFE HISTORY OF THE UNITED STATES

SERIES EDITOR *Sam Welles*

ASSISTANT EDITOR *Harold C. Field*

DESIGNER *Frank Crump*

STAFF WRITERS *Peter Meyerson, Tim Carr*

CHIEF RESEARCHER *Clara E. Nicolai*

RESEARCHERS *Patricia Tolles, Mary-Jo Kline, Jacqueline Coates, Evelyn Hauptman, Mary Youatt, Ellen Leiman, Natalia Zunino, Malabar Brodeur, Lilla Zabriskie*

PICTURE RESEARCHERS *Margaret K. Goldsmith, Joan Scafarello*

ART ASSOCIATE *Robert L. Young*

ART ASSISTANTS *James D. Smith, Wayne R. Young, Douglas B. Graham*

COPY STAFF *Marian Gordon Goldman, Gail Weesner, Dolores A. Littles*

PUBLISHER *Rhett Austell*

GENERAL MANAGER *John A. Watters*

LIFE MAGAZINE

EDITOR   MANAGING EDITOR   PUBLISHER
Edward K. Thompson   *George P. Hunt*   *Jerome S. Hardy*

Valuable assistance in the preparation of this volume was given by Roger Butterfield, who was picture consultant; Doris O'Neil, Chief of the LIFE Picture Library; Clara Applegate of the TIME-LIFE News Service; and Content Peckham, Chief of the Time Inc. Bureau of Editorial Reference.

THE COVER shows a Yank battling Germans on the Western Front in World War I. More than two million doughboys were sent to France, signaling America's emergence as a world power. The painting also appears on page 24.

CONTENTS

1. FORCE WITHOUT STINT OR LIMIT

ON the morning of April 3, 1917, the news spread through Europe that President Woodrow Wilson on the previous night had asked Congress to declare war on Germany. The German government took the news philosophically, unshaken in its judgment that the United States could not arm fast enough to alter the course of the war. The embattled Allies unanimously applauded Wilson's resolution. In Paris American flags sprouted in windows and bedecked the full length of the great boulevards. From London American Ambassador Walter Page reported that Foreign Minister Arthur Balfour "shook my hand warmly and said: 'It's a great day for the world,'" and when Wilson's name was mentioned in the House of Commons, the members burst into applause.

In Washington, D.C., the opinions of politicians were far from unanimous. Former President Theodore Roosevelt, who had long been demanding U.S. intervention in Europe, exultantly told reporters, "The President's message is a great state paper." Robert M. La Follette of Wisconsin battled vainly against Wilson's resolution in the Senate on April 4, then damned the war from beginning to end. In the midnight hours of April 5-6, when the roll was being called in the House, Representative Jeannette Rankin of Montana rose to her feet and said in a shaking voice, "I want to stand by my country, but I cannot vote for war." But the headlines in the morning newspapers attested that war had come to America: "HOUSE, AT 3:12 A.M., VOTES FOR WAR, 373

READY FOR BATTLE, this infantryman (the slang word for him was "doughboy") epitomizes the U.S. role in World War I. More than a million Americans saw action in France.

The pacifist movement was infuriated by war's degradation of the human intellect. In this 1915 cartoon by Robert Minor, an elated Army medical examiner views an inductee with great brawn but no head. "At last," the examiner sighs happily, "a perfect soldier!" This is but one of hundreds of antiwar cartoons that appeared in America before the declaration of war.

TO 50; $3,000,000,000 ASKED FOR ARMY OF 1,000,000; NATION'S GIGANTIC RESOURCES MOBILIZED." Three-time presidential candidate William Jennings Bryan, who had cried that the United States should never "get down and wallow in the mire of human blood," was heartsick; but he bravely wired the White House that he would serve as a private if called, and that until then he would "contribute to the comfort of soldiers in the hospitals and . . . aid in safeguarding the morals of the men in camp."

The initial reaction of the American people was unenthusiastic, even unexcited. Large numbers of Midwesterners, particularly in regions that were heavily German-American, were disgruntled. In the big cities people showed little more than routine patriotism at first. Hardened by the long succession of war crises, Americans were inclined to wait calmly until the government announced what would be required of them. For the moment not even Congress knew what the war would entail. According to one report, when Thomas S. Martin of the Senate Finance Committee asked why the Army needed three billion dollars, he was told, "We might have to send an army to France, and in that case we should want it ready." "Good Lord!" replied the senator. "You aren't going to send soldiers over there, are you?"

Soldiers—along with huge loans—were exactly what the Allies needed most: In 32 months of fighting they had lost most of a generation—in two 1916 battles alone, some 420,000 Englishmen were casualties at the Somme and 460,000 Frenchmen at Verdun. Both nations quickly dispatched war missions to Washington—England's under Arthur Balfour, France's under former Premier René Viviani. The most notable member of Viviani's mission was portly Marshal Joseph Joffre, who had commanded France's desperate stand along the Marne in 1914. Joffre, widely known as "Papa," made a modest request: He asked that one American division be sent to France at once to bolster his nation's sagging morale. Wilson agreed.

ACTUALLY, in April 1917 the United States was so poorly prepared for war that it could not claim a single organized division. To fulfill Joffre's request, five regiments had to be hastily assembled to approximate a division's 28,000-man strength. The whole Army numbered only 200,000, most of them recent enlistments in early stages of training. And as yet no officer had been selected to command an American expeditionary force.

To some military men, the logical candidate for the post was Major General Leonard Wood, a tough, opinionated veteran with a fine record. The most significant of Wood's contributions was an experimental camp that he set up at Plattsburg, New York, in 1915; it became the model for a system of officers' training schools, urgently needed in 1917 to turn out "90-day wonders" as leaders for America's expanding Army. But General Wood was promptly eliminated because he had a bad leg and because he had indiscreetly called President Wilson a "spineless rabbit." John J. Pershing, the only general to receive serious consideration, won the appointment as commander of the American Expeditionary Force.

To many men who served with him, Pershing seemed to be a spit-and-polish officer who judged every soldier by the standards of training and discipline at West Point. As correspondent Heywood Broun later commented, it was clear that no one would ever call him "Papa Pershing."

But this grim-faced six-footer was far more than a disciplinarian. Pershing had been better educated than most cadets arriving at West Point, and he had not stopped learning after he left the academy. As a cavalry lieutenant in the Indian wars, he took the trouble to study Apache dialects. Later he used his spare time to take a law degree. During his service in the Philippine insurrection, he again mastered native tongues. (The only language that ever gave him trouble was, ironically, French.) He had been among the first officers picked for the General Staff when that corps was set up in 1903.

Pershing had proved his efficiency in the field. In the West and in Cuba he had served well with Negro units, which later suggested his nickname, "Black Jack." In the peacetime army, with its rigid seniority system, Pershing was still a captain at 46, but he was so highly regarded that President Roosevelt jumped him to brigadier general, passing over 852 senior officers.

After he got his star, Pershing proved himself a first-class military governor in the Philippines and an effective administrator in posts at home. His 35 years of service had taught him much about handling men, and his dozen years in the limelight had added luster to his natural prudence and complete reliability. His chief of staff, General James G. Harbord, later summed him up: "General Pershing is a very strong character. . . . He is playing for high stakes and does not intend to jeopardize his winnings. . . . He is extremely cautious, very cautious, does nothing hastily or carelessly. . . . He does not fear responsibility, with all his caution. He decides big things more quickly than he does trivial ones. . . ."

ON May 10, 1917, Pershing arrived in Washington to lay plans and choose personnel for his staff. He observed that "The War Department seemed to be suffering from a kind of inertia, for which it was perhaps not altogether responsible." Overcoming the inertia was only one of the problems that faced Secretary of War Newton D. Baker. This small, dapper man, a former pacifist who had been mayor of Cleveland, was hard at work preparing for the great expansion of the Army.

Pershing's headquarters group grew rapidly. On May 27 he bade his farewells and received orders officially designating him commander in chief of the American Expeditionary Force. Significantly, Baker's orders stipulated that, while Pershing was to co-operate fully with the Allies, "the underlying idea must be kept in view that the forces of the United States are a separate and distinct component of the combined forces, the identity of which must be preserved." This principle would be strongly contested by the Allies in the months to come.

On May 28, amid a flurry of conspicuous secrecy, Pershing and his 187-man party sailed from New York harbor aboard the British liner *Baltic*. After four busy days in England, they crossed the Channel to France and were welcomed to Paris on June 13.

During Pershing's round of war talks, he was pressed to take part in a Franco-American Fourth of July celebration. The general reluctantly summoned to Paris a detachment from the A.E.F.'s token vanguard. On July 4 huge crowds cheered the troops wildly, but French military men were quick to note that the Americans were ill-equipped and that they marched poorly, in ragged ranks and files. Said one observer: "If this is what we may expect from America, the war is lost. These men are not soldiers; they are a uniformed rabble."

From isolated farm communities to the biggest cities, posters like the one above greeted the public with patriotic slogans urging support for the war effort. Combining the talents of America's finest artists and leading advertising men, the fund-raising campaigns produced spectacular results: In five bond drives alone, the posters helped to net the government $21.5 billion.

After this inauspicious debut, Pershing hurried his raw troops into training areas behind quiet sectors of the front, and as soon as he could, he moved his headquarters to Chaumont, an old provincial town about 150 miles east of Paris. Thus, in relative seclusion, Pershing began the prodigious task of building an American army in France.

A home the American people moved slowly from watchful waiting to willing participation. From week to week the change was imperceptible; but before the declaration of war, the people had been singing the pacifist song, "I Didn't Raise My Boy to Be a Soldier," and six months later they were singing George M. Cohan's rousing martial tune, "Over There."

The government decided that the A.E.F. was to be composed mainly of draftees rather than volunteers. The decision took courage. In the Philippine campaign, the only time that American soldiers had served outside the Western Hemisphere, all the troops had been volunteers; and the only American attempt at conscription had led to the large-scale Civil War draft riots. Yet on the whole the public seemed undismayed. In fact many were concerned that a selective-service system which tried to keep essential workers in civilian jobs might deny some patriots a chance to fight.

The first Selective Service Act passed Congress on May 17 by an overwhelming vote. Under the act, all men aged 21 to 30 were to register. A man with dependents or an essential job such as farm work could be deferred by a board made up of people from his locality. To meet one objection to the draft, volunteering was also permitted. Almost 10 million men registered in 1917. By war's end, with the age limits extended to 18 and 45, over 24 million would register. Of these 4.8 million volunteered or were called up. Minor resistance in some farm districts was the only sign of opposition to the draft.

Actually, draft officials received a good deal of unsolicited assistance. Vigilante bands, formed in various cities to hunt down "slackers," staged raids on theaters, pool halls and baseball parks. Every man who looked fit for service had to show a draft card. Often men too old or too young to register were carted off to armories and police stations. Of the thousands arrested only a minute percentage turned out to be draft dodgers.

The excesses of extremist groups tended to confirm a prophecy made by President Wilson before war was declared. "Once lead this people into war," he had said, "and they'll forget there ever was such a thing as tolerance. To fight you must be brutal and ruthless, and the spirit of ruthless brutality will enter into the very fiber of our national life."

Wilson himself implemented this grim view in his efforts to rouse public opinion. While he stressed America's noble aims, the President exhorted the people to wage the war with passion, calling for "Force to the utmost, Force without stint or limit." Wilson's Administration did not stint in the use of its powers. The Postmaster General banned from the mails such periodicals as the left-wing *Masses*, the anti-English *Bull* and the *Jeffersonian*, which criticized the war effort. Congress passed espionage, sabotage and sedition acts that outlawed, among other things, "disloyal, profane, scurrilous, or abusive" language against the government. Under these acts the Attorney General sent to prison "Big Bill" Haywood, a leader of the radical Industrial Workers of the World, Socialist spokesman Eugene V. Debs and many smaller fry. Charles T. Schenck, a Socialist convicted of distributing an antidraft tract, appealed to

Even before America entered the war, Girl Scouts were actively supporting the Allies. Among many other projects, they collected peach stones (above) to be burned and made into charcoal for gas-mask filters. A British general, praising them for their contributions, added cautiously that "there is no need for them . . . to drop their prime duties as home keepers and mothers."

the Supreme Court. But Justice Oliver Wendell Holmes upheld the conviction, ruling that "The character of every act depends upon the circumstances in which it is done. . . . The most stringent protection of free speech would not protect a man in falsely shouting fire in a theater and causing a panic. . . . The question in every case is whether the words are used in such circumstances and are of such a nature as to create a clear and present danger."

The stern policies set by the federal government had some unfortunate echoes. Thousands of volunteers collected gossip about alleged disloyalty and passed it along to the Justice Department. A Committee of Public Information distributed millions of pieces of inflammatory propaganda; this literature, along with the committee's traveling speakers, attacked pacifists and fostered the popular opinion that radicals who opposed the war were in league with the enemy. Many responsible Americans felt obliged to overstate their patriotism in order to avoid charges of disloyalty. State governments passed repressive laws that punished radical agitators. Although other laws were passed to forestall violence, they did not come in time to prevent atrocities. In Butte, Montana, a crowd lynched an I.W.W. organizer, and in Bisbee, Arizona, citizens rounded up more than 1,000 I.W.W.-led strikers, herded them into cattle cars and dumped them in the New Mexico desert without food or water.

War hysteria reached its peak in the protracted persecution of millions of German-Americans. Few of these "hyphenated" Americans were proved guilty of disloyal acts, and many served gallantly with the A.E.F., but all were suspected. In some secondary schools the study of German was abolished. Some extremists signed pledges never again to buy German products. At certain war-bond rallies, a few German-Americans were forced to march as objects of scorn and abuse.

Wheatless and meatless days— "Hooverizing"—were a part of the campaign waged by U.S. Food Administrator Herbert Hoover (above) to persuade Americans to impose voluntary limits on their consumption of vital commodities. He insisted on voluntary programs rather than rationing because, he said, "Americans are the most cooperative people in the world."

BUT most Americans expressed their growing commitment to war in more constructive ways. The challenge they faced was a staggering one. The A.E.F. had to be equipped, transported to France, supplied and maintained. The estimate of troops needed for battle kept increasing—from a half-million to one million to two million and more. While America was raising these forces, it had to send to the Allies a continuous flow of food and munitions. Americans not only had to make the tools of war but in many cases they had to build the factories to make the tools.

The people gave of their money. The personal income tax, enacted in 1913, had been applied only to single people making more than $3,000 and married people earning more than $4,000; the rates ranged from 1 per cent in the lowest bracket to 7 per cent in the highest. In wartime the tax was extended to cover every income over $1,000 (or $2,000 for married couples); and rates were raised to 4 per cent at the bottom and 67 per cent at the top. This tax, plus corporation taxes, a graduated war-profits levy and increased excises, yielded the government almost $3.7 billion in 1918. Voluntary purchases of Liberty bonds, Victory bonds, war savings certificates and thrift stamps totaled $23 billion—this from a population with an average annual income of less than $70 billion.

The people gave of their time. Though nearly five million men eventually went into uniform and the pool of unemployed in 1917 was under two million, the shortage of labor was made up. Some of the new workers were elderly people, some housewives. Of course most of them earned good pay, but the fact remained that they did not have to take jobs. Many others volunteered for nonpaying war work. The Red Cross, the Y.M.C.A., the Knights of Columbus, the National Jewish Welfare Board and the Salvation Army sent groups to serve overseas. Workers from these and similar organizations swarmed about training camps in America handing out refreshments, putting on church services, shows and dances. Film stars tried to outdo each other in selling war bonds. Almost everyone was eager to do his bit.

The people disciplined themselves. Told that the Army and the Allies needed food, they pledged themselves to meatless and wheatless days. Warned that wage rises might bring inflation and jeopardize the war effort, workers kept their demands to a minimum. Working through a War Labor Board in Washington, Samuel Gompers of the AFL helped avoid strikes. Never before had the whole nation risen up with such purpose and such zeal.

As chairman of the War Industries Board, Bernard Baruch controlled American industry quietly and effectively. He rarely clashed with businessmen—but he openly and heartily damned profiteers. His wartime works gained him "a reputation worth more than his millions, and earned more hardly."

BUT energy and enthusiasm could accomplish little without organization. Strong direction had to come from a government oriented to represent the public rather than to control it. Politicians had to learn to give orders.

At first the Administration relied on exhortation. For the food-saving campaign, the President called in Herbert Hoover, who had headed a successful relief program in Belgium. Hoover gathered a corps of volunteers who toured the country urging the people to cut down on meat and bread consumption, to eat more corn and spinach, and to observe "the gospel of the clean plate." Wilson also appointed individuals and commissions to preach conservation of fuel, raw materials and transportation facilities.

Despite earnest public co-operation, voluntary efforts were not enough. In the foreseeable future, there would not be enough food to meet all needs. Hoover had to be empowered to decide what proportion of farm products should go into government bins for shipment to the Army and the Allies. Since this meant cutting into the civilian supply, thus increasing the demand and risking inflation, he also had to have control over prices. He was not given the power to tell farmers what crops and how much they should grow; but by setting reasonably high prices, he stimulated the production of essential foodstuffs. Similar controls were placed on fuels. Wilson named as fuel administrator Harry Garfield, president of Williams College, and empowered him to start rationing.

Snowballing chaos in transportation led Wilson to appoint William McAdoo as director-general of railroads. At the same time he was Secretary of the Treasury, director of Liberty Loans, soldiers' insurance and the Federal Reserve Board, inspiring the pun "McAdoo's work is never McAdone."

After failing by all other means to straighten out transportation snarls, Wilson made his most drastic move of the war, taking over all of the nation's railroads and putting them under a railroad co-ordinator, Secretary of the Treasury William G. McAdoo. (Under the law, the railroads were to revert to private ownership after the war; but government management proved so efficient and won so many supporters that it took a determined fight by railroad executives to bring about denationalization.) The government went into business in other ways—for example, building and operating a nitrate plant at Muscle Shoals in the Tennessee Valley.

Regulatory systems were greatly expanded. Ultimately the Overman Act of May 1918 authorized the President to delegate his emergency powers to any individuals or agencies he chose. (A Republican senator sarcastically proposed an amendment to this bill: "If any power, constitutional or not, has been inadvertently omitted from this bill, it is hereby granted in full.") Anticipating the law, Wilson strengthened his War Industries Board in March 1918, endowing it with power to determine priorities for production materials and to recommend the prices for government purchases of supplies. What the food, fuel and railroad administrations did in their lines, the War Industries Board did wholesale, eventually forming some 60 sections to control industries as varied as chemicals, farm machinery and woolens.

THE chairman of this board, Bernard M. Baruch, was practically an economic dictator. To some his profession made him a peculiar choice. In 1917, when Baruch was asked by a congressional committee to state his occupation, he had answered simply, "I am a speculator." He had made a fortune in Wall Street, betting on the rise and fall of stocks.

But Wilson had known what he was about. Baruch had a computerlike mind. At the brokerage house where he served his apprenticeship, the partners did not consult indexes of financial statistics; young Bernie could give them company data more quickly and just as accurately. Wilson called him "Dr. Facts," and all the facts in his storehouse were relevant to his job. He knew which companies' production estimates were accurate and which men to call in order to get swift action. Best of all, Baruch and the President knew each other. They had met in 1912, and since October 1916 Baruch had been an adviser to Wilson, never questioning his decisions and never asking a reward. His feeling for the President approached reverence, and Wilson reciprocated with trust. Once when Baruch started to explain a decision, Wilson interrupted, saying "You don't have to explain. Our minds have met and I have the utmost confidence in your judgment." Baruch could count on support from the White House in any decision he made, and everyone knew it.

As chairman of the War Industries Board, Baruch never abused his power, and only on rare occasions did he threaten force. Once, to bring into line some automobile manufacturers who refused to curtail passenger-car production, Baruch let them listen as he telephoned the railroad administrator and suspended train service to their plants. Next he called the Secretary of War and asked that the Army seize the car companies' stockpiles of steel. After his third call, the General Motors man stopped him and said, "I quit." The others followed suit.

Most of the time Baruch relied on persuasion. On his team were journalists, military men and professors of economics; but most of its members were successful financiers and businessmen such as Leland Summers of J. P. Morgan and Company, Alexander Legge of International Harvester and George N. Peek of Deere and Company. Dealing chiefly with other businessmen, they talked the same language and won co-operation through salesmanship. American businessmen, said Baruch, were ready "to do whatever was required of them when they knew why."

Partly because production was delayed by factory construction and the training of workmen, partly because the government was slow in shifting from exhortation to command, there were failings in the industrial effort. Most new shipping did not come off the ways until it was no longer needed; more than half of America's troops reached Europe in English ships. Aircraft production also failed to get going in time, and American airmen fought almost exclusively in planes of French and British manufacture. Throughout the war most of the artillery used by the A.E.F. was supplied by France.

Newton Baker, Wilson's Secretary of War, was accused of ineptitude and of running the War Department to bolster his ego. He was in fact a competent man faced with unprecedented problems of modern warfare. "War," he said, "is no longer David with his sling; it is the conflict of smokestacks now."

Yet the output of U.S. factories was prodigious. Wartime production included 9.5 million Army overcoats, 34 million pairs of shoes, 3.1 million rifles, 5.4 million gas masks, 22 million blankets, and a torrent of trucks, locomotives, communications and maintenance equipment. Never before had the world seen such a display of industrial might.

IN the fall of 1917 it seemed unlikely that the nation's strength could be brought to bear on the battlefield in time to stave off Allied disaster. German armies on the Eastern Front had driven Russia to the brink of collapse. German and Austrian forces inflicted a smashing defeat on the Italians at Caporetto in October and November. The Allied merchant fleets were overtaxed by the mounting volume of American war production, and in the Atlantic, German submarines took a heavy toll. Admiral William S. Sims, the commander of U.S. naval forces in Europe, had persuaded the British Admiralty to organize transports into convoys, thus reducing losses; but the U-boat menace would not be brought under control until the spring of 1918.

Meanwhile training camps in America bulged with restless soldiers. The early waves of inductees had swamped existing facilities. The shortage of uniforms forced innumerable soldiers to start their training in civilian clothes. Until there were enough rifles to go around, many men had to drill with broomsticks. Though such deficiencies were at first counterbalanced by enthusiasm, soldiers soon grew bored with inactivity. Under the familiar evangelists' sign "Where will you spend eternity?" one recruit scrawled, "At Camp McClellan." Only 175,000 Americans had reached France by the end of 1917.

While Pershing imperturbably pressed his plans for an American army, the Allies' bleak military prospects caused upheavals in France and England. In November 1917 a government shake-up in Paris brought to power as prime minister Georges Clemenceau, a tough old fighter who had been known as "the Tiger" of French politics for more than a generation. In November too the Allies finally acknowledged that separate commands could not effectively conduct a vast and complex war. In a conference at Rapallo the Allied leaders set up an international control body—the Supreme War Council.

Clemenceau and David Lloyd George, England's brilliant prime minister, were dominant figures in this council. They were committed to inter-Allied co-operation; but each was dedicated first to the best interests of his own country. Since Clemenceau and Lloyd George were reluctant to gamble their nations' fate on a green American army, they opposed Pershing's efforts to establish an autonomous force. Pershing had previously been promised an American front by General Henri Philippe Pétain, the commander in chief of the French armies; but now he found himself fighting for the life of his unborn army. French and British generals joined Clemenceau and Lloyd George in demanding American troops to fill out the ranks of their depleted armies. Pershing occasionally sent a regiment or a division to the French or British rear areas for training, but he doggedly insisted that these outfits were on temporary loan and that he would reclaim them just as soon as an American army was ready to take over its own front and fight its own battles.

Pershing was just as determined that the A.E.F. should fight in its own way. Since the battle of the Marne in 1914, the Allies and Germans had been fighting from trenches. Between the enemy lines lay no man's land, visited only by snipers and occasional patrols. Behind rows of trenches and barbed

Every Man!

Between the ages of 18 to 45 [both inclusive], except those previously registered,

Must Register

FOR THE

Selective Service Draft

SEPTEMBER 12

1918

→Penalty for Failure to Register←

is one year imprisonment, and NO man can exonerate himself by the payment of a fine.

Patriots Will Register~Others Must

REGISTER PROMPTLY!

Although conscription was generally accepted with a good-natured shrug, there were numerous draft dodgers. One of them, Grover Cleveland Bergdoll, was so notorious as "the super slacker of all" that relatives changed their names to escape the bad odor. He fled to Germany where he was received as a celebrity. Bergdoll's mother exclaimed "He is one foolish boy!"

wire were deeper, more permanent works which provided the bulk of the armies with some shelter against bombardment or gas attack. Operations consisted in the main of short, costly rushes against enemy trenches. Even successful attacks seldom netted more than a few acres. The prevailing theory of trench warfare was that the other side would eventually exhaust its strength and have to sue for terms. Meanwhile millions of men squatted in deep mud or icy water, suffered lice and rats, endured the acrid smells of exploded gunpowder and human wastes, the persistent boom and rattle of gunfire. Men lost their minds in this nightmarish landscape. Those who recovered usually explained, "It was the noise, the endless noise."

Pershing wanted no part of this kind of warfare. He wanted the American Army to move and fight in the open. It even displeased him to have French and British veterans assigned as A.E.F. instructors, for he feared that they would teach defensive tactics. The Allied generals thought him naïve, as, in some respects, he was. Many of his ideas were to be modified by experience, but he remained wedded to the conviction that "victory could not be won by the costly process of attrition, but it must be won by driving the enemy out into the open and engaging him in a war of movement."

PERSHING spared no effort to keep the A.E.F. adequately supplied. To deliver food and munitions quickly to the front and to ensure a continuous flow after fighting began, he and his staff developed the vast and elaborate Services of Supply. This organization built its own dock facilities at various ports, laid 1,000 miles of railroad, put up refrigeration and baking plants and even built candy factories. Another supply group, the General Purchasing Board, operated from Paris, buying in Europe what could be gotten there. At the head of it was a big, blustering Chicago banker, Charles G. Dawes, whose vivid vocabulary later earned him the nickname "Hell and Maria."

Ultimately the problems of supply became so complex that Washington thought of establishing a separate command to handle them. General George Goethals, the builder of the Panama Canal, was suggested as the head of the supply organization. Pershing fought the plan, insisting that he retain all responsibility. The A.E.F. commander won; eventually he delegated command of the Services of Supply to General Harbord. Pershing continued to improve the supply network while seeing to it that his gathering combat forces were drilled incessantly and put through the paces of offensive campaigning.

Life was not all hard work for the doughboys in training in France. After hours, the Yanks fraternized with neighboring Allied troops, learned to enjoy French wines and English humor. They took part in team games and boxing matches. They conducted raids to steal firewood from under the noses of the officials whom French towns appointed to guard their precious supply. There were sights to see on trips to mobile delousing units. There were the gay days of leave in Dijon and Aix-les-Bains and—best of all—Paris. Many an American received a liberal education in the streets and historic buildings of Paris; there was truth as well as sentiment in the popular postwar song: "How 'ya gonna keep 'em down on the farm, after they've seen Par-ee!"

The A.E.F. did little fighting in 1917. In October an artillery commander just east of Nancy insisted on firing a barrage at the Germans in spite of the French, who prized the quietness of the sector. In November three infantrymen of the 1st Division were killed near the same spot. But through

This Is A Loaf of Bread And A Dol-lar Bill. If You Were A-lone On A Des-ert Is-land And Starv-ing To Death, Which Would You Rather Have? The Dol-lar Would Mean Noth-ing To You Then. The Bread Would Mean Ev-er-y-thing. Which Shows, Dear Child-ren, That In The Fin-al An-al-y-sis Mon-ey Is Nothing. On-ly Life Real-ly Mat-ters. Give Your Mon-ey Now To Save Your Life Later.

James Montgomery Flagg was a talented artist whose work as a war propagandist was outstanding. He directed this successful "reading exercise" at children in a pamphlet urging them to buy Liberty Bonds. Flagg later wrote: "I believe that neither women nor noble ideals primarily influence men to go to war, but that they fight because men are fighting animals."

all the bitter cold winter, Americans saw service only in peaceful areas.

Not until the spring of 1918 did the A.E.F. have a half-million men. But by then England was using many of its vessels to transport American troops, and the monthly shipping rate was building up steadily toward its peak of 300,000 men in July. Now the Yanks were pouring ashore at French ports. They came laden with new gear, half-trained but eager. They were, said an English military man, "the last great reserve army of civilization."

As the strength of the A.E.F. increased, so did Allied demands upon it. Pershing released as few units as he could. It was the Germans, not the Allies, who forced Pershing's hand on the manpower issue.

In March 1918 at Brest Litovsk, the Imperial German government wrung a separate peace from the new Communist government of Russia, freeing German troops from the Eastern armies for service on the Western Front. Erich Ludendorff, the daring general who was now virtual dictator in Germany, rushed many of these men west to take part in a great offensive. On March 21 he struck with massed artillery and infantry against the point where the 300-mile French line adjoined the 100-mile British front. Hurdling the bodies of fallen comrades, 64 German divisions broke the Allied trench defenses and cut a swath 50 miles wide and up to 37 miles deep. The English were in danger of being trapped with their backs to the sea; the French might lose the roads to Paris—and Paris itself.

This desperate crisis forced the Allies to establish closer co-operation between their distinct national armies. The Supreme War Council, in an emergency session on March 26, created the post of Allied military co-ordinator. The officer appointed to the post was General Ferdinand Foch, a short, wrinkled, bristling Frenchman who was fiercely dedicated to the army and the study of warfare. (On April 24 the council went a step further and designated Foch the supreme commander of all Allied forces in Europe.) In Foch, Pershing faced the strongest opponent to his plans for forming an American army.

THE German threat left Pershing no choice. On March 28 he drove to visit Foch in his headquarters. In the garden of a farmhouse, under a new-blooming cherry tree, Pershing declared in his best French: "I am here to say that the American people would consider it a great honor for our troops to be engaged in the present battle. I ask it of you in my name and theirs. There is at the moment no other question but of fighting. Infantry, artillery, aviation —all that we have are yours. Use them as you will."

Nothing came of the offer: Foch, for reasons known only to himself, did not use the American divisions at this critical moment. Fortunately the first German offensive stalled some 40 miles from Paris. In the second week of April, when Ludendorff struck again, it was farther to the northwest, against the British in the Lys Valley. At this point Foch did assign the Americans a divisional area north of Paris, opposite the village of Cantigny, where the previous German offensive had made its deepest penetration.

Before there was serious fighting at Cantigny, American troops met their first test of battle elsewhere—with disastrous results. On the night of April 20-21 the Germans staged a surprise raid against a quiet training area in the Lorraine region. At the village of Seicheprey German shock troops fell on three companies of the 26th (Yankee) Division and nearly wiped them out, inflicting some 650 casualties.

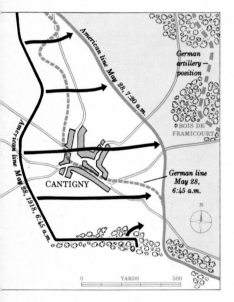

THE FIRST ATTACK:

CANTIGNY—MAY 28, 1918

Advancing under a heavy artillery barrage, approximately 4,000 Yanks of the 1st Division stormed Cantigny in the first American offensive action of the war. Against sporadic resistance they quickly took their limited objectives on the first day, May 28, 1918. Then German infantrymen counterattacked violently, almost cracking the new American line. Several times in three days German assaults were repulsed. The Americans suffered fairly heavy casualties, and the victory was of little strategic importance. But Cantigny proved to the Allies that the Yanks could fight.

Through German propaganda agencies, news of this coup was promptly and widely circulated. American publicists retorted that the attackers had been driven back and called Seicheprey a victory. But the American press was plainly upset. The New York *Herald* suggested that the Germans had resorted to dope to "bestialize" their troops. The American fighting man seemed to have been measured and found wanting.

The Yanks' poor showing at Seicheprey, coupled with heavy British casualties in the Lys Valley, spurred the Allied leaders to redouble their resistance to the American plan for a separate army. In a May meeting the Supreme War Council put Pershing under relentless pressure. General Foch, along with Clemenceau and Lloyd George, not only demanded American troops as replacements, but specified infantry and machine-gun units exclusively. Pershing steadfastly defended his program of assembling complete divisions. Foch asked, "You are willing to risk our being driven back to the Loire?" Pershing replied grimly, "Yes, I am willing to take the risk. Moreover, the time may come when the American Army will have to stand the brunt of this war, and it is not wise to fritter away our resources in this manner." Moments later, Pershing overheard a British war minister whisper to Lloyd George, "You can't budge him an inch."

EAGER to prove the mettle of American troops, Pershing and his staff prepared for a local offensive at Cantigny. The 1st Division, which had the assignment at Cantigny, consisted mainly of regulars, and it was ahead of the other divisions in its training. Its commander, General Robert Lee Bullard, had been hand-picked by Pershing for his aggressiveness. Its operations officer, responsible for tactical plans, was Colonel George Catlett Marshall, who at 37 had already been singled out as a comer even though he had graduated from Virginia Military Institute and not West Point. Pershing saw to it that what the division lacked was supplied by the French—artillery, flame throwers and some of the small, awkward tanks just then coming into use. With these resources, the 1st was to take the offensive.

Cantigny itself was on a hilltop overlooking woods and shell-torn farms. The village was a difficult place to attack, but its German garrison was weak, made up of troops unfit to be used on the offensive.

On May 27 the 1st Division wriggled into final positions a mile from Cantigny. At dawn on the 28th some 4,000 Americans of the 1st received the order, "Come on, boys." A deadly artillery barrage kept moving about 25 yards ahead of their front ranks. Across the chewed-up ground they moved—infantry, machine-gun companies and tanks together. Before the Germans could fully man their guns, Americans were in the streets of the village. Flame throwers seared the defenders out of their positions. Cantigny was captured.

But the battle was not yet won. Time and again German forces counterattacked. One dangerous advance was driven back by a battalion under the command of Lieutenant Colonel Theodore Roosevelt Jr. By May 30 the last enemy thrust had been repelled. Although the 1st Division had suffered 1,067 casualties, Cantigny could be chalked up as a victory—the first in the war for American troops, the first ever won by Americans fighting in Europe. It went a long way toward wiping out the bitter memory of Seicheprey, at least in the minds of the A.E.F. But the war had scarcely started for the American Army. The Yanks had a hard and bloody road to travel.

General John J. Pershing, "the soldier nobody knew," was once characterized as a man who "could no more laugh than a stone image." But Pershing was far from being an unemotional man. Shortly after America entered the war, he said, "It is horrible beyond the power of words to express, to think that the civilized world should suffer such bloodshed and destruction."

A joint session of Congress listens, on April 2, 1917, while President Wilson urges it to declare war.

For the Yanks are coming

THE conflict into which America was finally drawn on April 6, 1917, was a modern war that utilized ancient forms of combat; a war in which individual heroism was ultimately overwhelmed by the technical superiority of mass-produced weapons. In France, from the North Sea to the Swiss border, the medieval strategy of siege warfare, with its stable fronts and field fortifications, was pursued with a panoply of traditional though improved weapons—rifles, bayonets, cannons and hand grenades—to which was added a deadly assortment of awesome new devices—machine guns, tanks, planes, poison gas and flame throwers. The result was a catastrophic loss of life as armies slugged each other into insensibility to gain or hold a few square yards of pulverized earth. By the time the doughboys of the American Expeditionary Force began manning the trenches, this policy of attrition, with its mass-produced death, had already cost millions of lives. The battles of the Somme, between July and November 1916, had resulted in more than 1,250,000 casualties with no decisive victory by either side.

This was the situation when the earliest troops of the A.E.F. arrived, the small initial group of 14,000 soldiers that would grow to an army of more than two million within 19 months. Although some congressional leaders predicted that these raw recruits would finish the war in six months and be back home for Christmas, it was soon apparent that a gigantic effort would be necessary before the world was presumably made "safe for democracy."

THIS COMPELLING POSTER by James Montgomery Flagg of Uncle Sam is almost a self-portrait of the artist. Millions of copies of this aid to recruiting were distributed.

I WANT YOU
FOR U.S.ARMY
NEAREST RECRUITING STATION

Marching in mufti, a patriotic group of New York businessmen does snappy squad drills in Battery Park during the lunch hour. The time is

Toughening up for combat, recruits of the 28th Division are put through the paces of strenuous calisthenics at Camp Hancock, Georgia.

April 1917, more than six weeks before the start of draft registration.

A resounding answer to the President's call to arms

COMPLIANCE with the Selective Service Act, which empowered President Wilson to enlist one million men including volunteers, was almost universal. Resistance was urged by dissident groups. If, said a Socialist paper, "war is Hell, then let those who want Hell go to Hell." Some 9.5 million men turned up at their local draft boards to register on June 5, 1917. General John J. Pershing, commander of the A.E.F., hoped to train recruits in six months at stateside work and three months of instruction in French camps and "quiet sectors" of the front. At the end of this preparation, Pershing expected that every soldier would feel "himself . . . invincible in battle." The response of draftees was noted by one officer: "The men show no apathy, and are not indignant at being drafted. . . . They feel . . . they are members of a National Army of their own creation. . . ."

Arriving in France, one of the first contingents of Yanks disembarks in June 1917 at Saint-Nazaire, a major port of entry for the A.E.F.

Fresh American units to turn the tide of battle

UNTIL the spring of 1918, when the bulk of the Americans saw their first action, there was time for hard training in the wintry fields of Lorraine and in the bleak Vosges Mountains. Rising at dawn and breakfasting on hardtack, a strip of bacon and a cup of weak coffee, the doughboys were relentlessly drilled both in defensive techniques of trench warfare and offensive tactics demanded by Pershing. The recruits learned to handle machine guns, lay barbed wire, hurl grenades, improve their marksmanship—and dig holes, the lesson taught by French veterans of three years of fighting. "A Frenchman never rested until he had dug a hole," said an American general. "And after that he never rested anywhere except in the hole." This training transformed "woefully ignorant" rookies into the fighting force whose exploits are recorded in these paintings and drawings.

WAITING TO ADVANCE during the Saint-Mihiel drive, troops rest in a shattered courtyard (above). The paintings here and on the following pages were done by American soldier-artists.

MOVING TO THE FRONT past a stream of refugees during the battle along the Aisne, an artillery detachment brings up a battery of guns over the road to Château-Thierry.

A sentry stands guard, his grenades neatly laid out before him. Grenades and flame throwers were preferred to rifles in trench warfare.

A BAYONET ATTACK on Blanc Mont is recorded by John W. Thomason Jr., a participant who wrote, "A few iron-souled Prussians . . . stood up to meet bayonet with bayonet, and died that way."

American troops overrun a German trench at Verdun in 1918. During the epochal fighting

STREET COMBAT, similar to the kind that took place at Château-Thierry, shows an American soldier standing over the body of a fallen buddy and firing at the enemy. The sketch is by Harvey Dunn.

Green troops in a murderous assault

THOUGH unseasoned, the German troops occupying Cantigny confidently awaited an expected American assault, the first Yankee offensive action of the war. "Only green American troops are opposing us," said the Germans. Then, on May 28, 1918, at 4:45 a.m., the 28th Infantry of the 1st Division launched its carefully staged attack. After an intensive artillery barrage, machine guns and mortars were brought up, and French-made Renault tanks, like those seen opposite, moved across the open fields. Following a precise timetable, a rolling barrage preceded the men as they advanced into the streets of the town. There they bayoneted the enemy in his trenches, seared him out of cellars, blasted him from shell holes with Mills grenades. By 7:20 a.m. the Germans had fled the town as all U.S. goals were reached.

in 1916, French troops rallied to the slogan, "They shall not pass," and lost 111,000 more men at Verdun than the A.E.F. lost from all causes.

Carrying camouflage nets, two Renault tanks climb a hill. The A.E.F. used these clumsy machines that often heated up to 140 degrees inside.

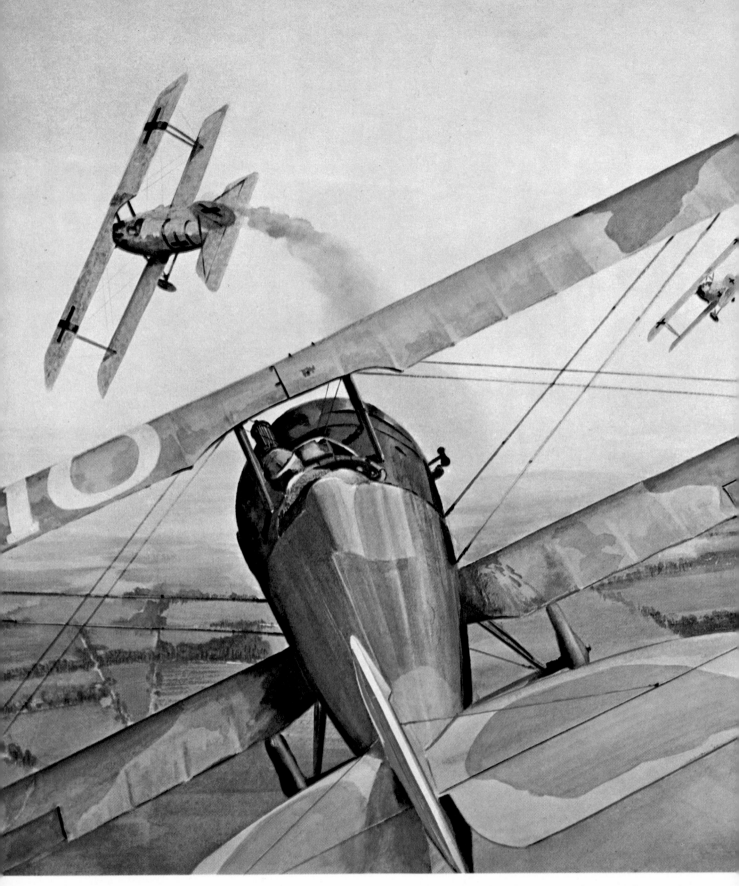

INITIAL TRIUMPHS by members of the famous 94th ("Hat in the Ring") Squadron of the First Pursuit Group are scored on April 18, 1918, when Lieutenants Douglas Campbell and Alan Winslow in French-built Nieuports down two German planes, one of which (above) is in flames. These were the first Germans shot down by Americans flying under their own flag.

AIRBORNE ARTILLERY in the form of the A.E.F.'s 96th Bombardment Squadron, the first Americans to bomb enemy territory, flies in formation for German targets on a daylight raid.

Knights-errant in flimsy flying machines

TRENCH warfare obliterated any lingering glamor of war. But the war in the air was a different matter. Flying frail, notoriously unreliable planes, the individual pilot preserved some of the dash of earlier chivalric warfare. The exploits of these heroes, who conquered or died (parachutes were not yet in use), were avidly followed by newspaper readers at home. In April 1916 the American volunteers who had joined the French Air Force were formed into the noted Lafayette Escadrille. Later, when the A.E.F. arrived, U.S. pilots made a more direct contribution to the air war, accounting for a total of 776 enemy aircraft while losing only 289. The premier American "ace," Eddie Rickenbacker alone shot down 21 German planes in the aerial dogfights.

ON DAWN PATROL, Captain Eddie Rickenbacker and Lieutenant Reed Chambers climb into the sky, planning to hover over a German airdrome and catch unwary pilots as they take off.

A WOUNDED DOUGHBOY is carried from a battlefield lit by flares. Two out of every hundred American fighting men died of disease or were killed; for each death, seven were wounded.

Above and beyond the call of duty

STUBBORN German resistance during the last great American offensive at Meuse-Argonne was the costliest to the A.E.F. in casualties. This victory produced many acts of individual heroism—Captain Sam Woodfill's exploit, less well known than some, is outstanding.

Shortly before he led his company through the Bois de la Pultière to take the town of Cunel, Woodfill, certain he would be killed, wrote a note asking that his wife be told that he had "fallen on the Field of Honor." Then he moved ahead across a field in which were sited four nests of German machine guns that were pinning down his men. One by one, the expert marksman picked off the five-man gun crews with his rifle. Moving in, Woodfill was attacked first by a soldier with a bayonet, then by an officer wielding a pistol. He shot them both with his pistol. Later as his men were crossing a muddy ravine, he advanced alone, took three prisoners and knocked out another nest. Now behind enemy lines, he killed two Germans with a pickax. Woodfill survived the battle and the war and got the Medal of Honor.

BETWEEN ASSAULTS, machine gunners rest. The 7th Machine Gun Battalion, in violent combat at Château-Thierry, turned back one of the last German offensives.

Silent guns and a "great carnival of peace"

WHEN peace finally came at 11 a.m. on November 11, 1918, men at the front halted in their tracks, built campfires against the cold and stretched out on the ground—strangely ill at ease now that the familiar sound of guns firing had ceased. Throughout the Allied nations, victory demonstrations began as soon as news of the armistice was heard. The roads to Paris were quickly clogged with pilgrims making their way to the Place de la Concorde to cheer, wave flags and embrace each other. Impromptu speeches on peace and the armistice were delivered by street orators. Soldiers of a dozen nationalities linked arms and joined the processions along the wide Champs Élysées. Overhead, Italian planes bombarded the revelers with flowers. In New York, once the news was spread, business was forgotten as thousands upon thousands of excited people poured into the streets in an almost somber demonstration of relief. One observer reported that "the mass of crowd . . . rarely raised a cheer or gave any other outward sign of rejoicing. It was enough to walk . . . streets with ten thousand strangers, and to realize that in that moment of good news not one of them was really a stranger."

A NAVY'S SURRENDER is seen in the painting by B. F. Gribble of the German High Seas Fleet being delivered to the victors, November 1918, at the Firth of Forth in Scotland.

ALLIED FLAGS in New York are displayed in George Luks's "Armistice Night, 1918." The confetti was so thick "a few matches would have set the business districts aflame."

2. TRIUMPH AND DISILLUSION

O<small>N</small> May 27, 1918, the day before the American 1st Division started its minor attack at Cantigny, General Erich Ludendorff launched Germany's third major offensive of the spring. In this massive blow, 360,000 German troops smashed the French lines at the Chemin Des Dames and poured through to the south. They gained 30 miles in 72 hours and reached the Marne River just 50 miles from Paris. Here the Allies had to duplicate the French stand of 1914. General Foch, encouraged by the Americans' victory at Cantigny, ordered the United States 2nd and 3rd Divisions up to the Marne.

These outfits, struggling forward over roads jammed with French military traffic and fleeing civilians, arrived at the river after the French had blunted the German onslaught. What remained for the Americans was the job of probing the enemy line to see if it could be pushed back. The sector assigned to the 2nd Division ran westward from Château-Thierry, where the German thrust had been checked. Its objective was to recapture a kidney-shaped thicket less than a mile wide and two miles deep—the Bois de Belleau, known to Americans as Belleau Wood.

Like Cantigny, this wood was on high ground with a view for miles around. But unlike Cantigny, its defenses were expertly laid out and manned by crack troops. Sown among its underbrush and outcroppings of rock were perfectly concealed machine-gun nests. Each nest had another machine gun covering it so that if one were taken, its captors would immediately be under

SEEKING PERMANENT PEACE, President Wilson (*left center*) participates in signing the Versailles Treaty in 1919. To his left in the Hall of Mirrors are France's Clemenceau and England's Lloyd George. The painting, by Sir William Orpen, is at London's Imperial War Museum.

fire. Mortars and artillery were zeroed in on outlying fields which the Americans would have to cross. Taking the wood promised to be a costly affair. The U.S. 2nd was a regular division. But the outfit was green: most of its personnel, including two regiments of Marines, were recent volunteers.

Under the command of General Harbord, whom Pershing had temporarily released from staff duty, the Marines made their first rush on Belleau Wood on June 6 and the greater part of two battalions was cut down. One unit, moving into a village, lost 380 out of 400 men. "The air was full of red-hot nails," wrote a reporter following the advance. The 2nd won a foothold at the edge of the wood, but many of the men found themselves pinned behind a moss-covered cliff. For six days they burrowed there, rushing out from time to time only to be driven back. So heavy was the German artillery fire that, as one Marine wrote, "the trees looked like someone had cut them down with a scythe."

Gradually American guns cut gaps in the enemy defenses, permitting parties of riflemen to creep into the wood. Nest by nest, the enemy was cleared out of the southernmost thickets, then the northeastern. Finally, after a 14-hour artillery barrage followed by a mass assault, the last corner of the wood was seized. The cost had been fearful—casualties approached 4,400. But Belleau Wood had the earmarks of a victory, and the French celebrated it with generosity by renaming the wood after the brigade of Marines.

From Belleau Wood on, there was no longer a question whether Americans could fight as well as Europeans. Twenty-five U.S. divisions were already in France; fresh ones were arriving at the rate of a division every few days, and Foch was ready to use them whenever Pershing would permit. The Germans, too, felt a new respect for Americans. The commander of the German corps which had faced the 2nd Division at Belleau Wood conceded that the outfit "must be considered a very good one and may even perhaps be reckoned as a storm troop. . . . The Americans' nerves are not yet worn out."

G ENERAL LUDENDORFF felt that Germany must deliver a knockout blow before too many American divisions reached the front. On July 15 he launched one more massive offensive. Marshaling every German unit and gun that could be spared, he threw many of them against the Château-Thierry sector, a lightly held part of the Marne salient. In front of the German spearhead stood only the understrength American 3rd Division, with a French unit on its right and the green-as-grass 28th Division in the rear.

The commander of the American regiment at the point of impact was Colonel Ulysses Grant McAlexander. Before the Germans attacked, he carefully laid out his defenses—rifle pits along the Marne, riflemen and machine gunners at the railroad embankment paralleling the river bank, others in shallow trenches covering the flanks. Just after midnight on July 15, the German artillery cut loose with shrapnel and poison gas shells. German infantry started filtering across the river in boats at about 2:30 a.m. McAlexander's entrenched Americans weathered the bombardment and turned back a patrol. But when the Germans attacked in force, they succeeded in bridging the river's 50-yard narrows with pontoons. The Americans met the Germans at the bank. With rifle, grenade, pistol, bayonet, trench knife and bare knuckles, the doughboys struggled to hold their positions. Up the river the 28th Division was bolstering the French line, and still farther up, the 42nd (Rainbow)

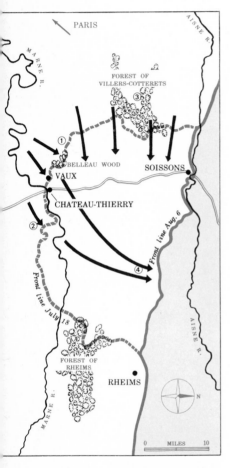

THE FINAL ASSAULT ON
THE GATEWAY TO PARIS

In their last breakthrough of the war, German troops advanced in May 1918 to a position threatening Paris, again occupying the Aisne-Marne salient, from which they had withdrawn four years earlier. French and American troops stopped the Germans at Belleau Wood (1) and pushed them back across the Marne (2). Meanwhile the German line was being pierced in the center by other units (3). Forced to give up the Soissons-Château-Thierry road, their major supply and escape route, the kaiser's forces fought a bitter retreat to a new defense line (4).

Division fought the attackers from trenches hastily cut into chalky soil.

None had to fight as McAlexander's regiment did. For over five hours the wheat fields on the banks of the Marne were a smoking inferno. A German lieutenant reported, "Never have I seen so many dead, never contemplated a spectacle of war so frightful. . . . [The] Americans in a hand-to-hand fight had completely annihilated two of our companies. Hidden in the wheat in a semi-circle, they had let our men advance, then had annihilated them with a fire at thirty or forty feet away. This enemy has coolness, one must acknowledge, but he gave proof that day of a bestial brutality. 'The Americans are killing everyone!' Such was the terrifying word that spread through all our ranks." McAlexander, with only 400 men left out of his original 1,500, finally had to pull back. But the Germans had had enough. They came no farther.

THE 3rd Division's stand at Château-Thierry—Pershing later called it "one of the most brilliant pages in our military annals"—had crippled Ludendorff's offensive before it could score any significant gain. German offensive strength was broken. With the Americans swinging the balance of manpower, the initiative on the Western Front had passed over to the Allies.

Ludendorff's last offensive had played directly into Foch's hands. Hoping to take the offensive before the Germans struck again, the Allied supreme commander had prepared plans for a series of local counteroffensives. The first of these was aimed at the vital town of Soissons, just a few miles inside the western flank of the very same Marne salient. If the Allies could take Soissons, they would cut the north-south railroad which supplied the Germans inside the salient; they would also deprive the enemy troops on the Marne of their best escape route. Unwittingly the Germans had co-operated with Foch's plan by vainly expending their strength around Château-Thierry while Foch was finishing his attack preparations some 20 miles to the north.

Foch assigned the command of the Soissons attack to France's most aggressive field general, Charles Mangin, "The Butcher." With the American 1st and 2nd Divisions and a French colonial division, Mangin was to push toward Soissons on a line paralleling the Aisne River. Meanwhile a bigger force, including most of four American divisions, would launch a holding action along the Marne, attempting to keep the Germans heavily engaged there until Mangin cut off their supply lines and escape routes. With luck, tens of thousands of the enemy might be trapped and forced to surrender.

For Mangin's offensive, men and munitions were brought up in utmost secrecy. Only men in key jobs knew what was up. Many of the troops first learned that a battle impended when word was passed that priests would hear confessions. On the night of July 17, in a driving rain, they moved to the edge of the forests. About an hour before dawn, they attacked.

Although preparatory shelling had been kept to a minimum in order not to alert the enemy, the guns had been well-aimed. The commander of the 1st Division was now General Charles P. Summerall, an artilleryman who knew how to use big guns. As a result many German emplacements had been knocked out of action, and in the first few hours Mangin's forces were able to drive two miles due east. Their objective, the Soissons-Château-Thierry road, was now only three miles distant.

But in those three miles were ravines and hilltops, bristling with hidden artillery, mortars, machine guns and infantry. Every step through this rough

1ST—"FIRST IN FRANCE"

26TH—YANKEE

42ND—RAINBOW

77TH—METROPOLITAN

92ND—BUFFALO

Most divisions in World War I proudly devised shoulder patches for identification. The 1st, a Regular Army outfit, used a bold red number 1. The 42nd chose a rainbow, signifying that it was made up of units from many states. The buffalo, emblem of the Negro 92nd, harked back to the Indian wars, when Negro troops wore buffalo skins to protect them from the cold.

terrain would cost lives, and Mangin's order was to pay the price. Wave after wave of riflemen rushed forward; machine guns chopped them down by the hundreds. Still they came, overpowering the enemy by sheer weight of numbers. The 2nd Division, now led by General Harbord, kept going until a quarter of its men were casualties and others were dropping from exhaustion. The tough 1st plowed on even longer, eventually losing 7,200 men. The French, mostly Senegalese with a sprinkling of men from the Foreign Legion, fought with equal valor, and so did the British troops thrown in when the Americans tired. By nightfall of July 19, the second day of the battle, Allied maps showed gouges cut more than five miles into the German flank near the northern base of the salient. The key highway was cut and barred.

THE Allied troops attacking along the Marne pushed northward in greater strength. The Germans opposite them, alert to the threat to their rear, started pulling back soon after the battle started. Although they had lost their best road north, they opened other routes and fought a bitter, orderly retreat. It would take the Allies days more and cost the Americans 50,000 casualties all told to wipe out the Marne salient, but the strategic phase of the campaign ended that July 18 at Soissons. German Chancellor Count von Hertling later said: "We expected grave events in Paris for the end of July. That was on the 15th. On the 18th even the most optimistic among us understood that all was lost. The history of the world was played out in three days."

Hard on the heels of the Soissons triumph, a British-led army attacked up near the Belgian border on August 8. Within a few days the Germans had been thrown back beyond positions they had held since 1914 and had lost more than 25,000 prisoners in the process. Ludendorff later called this shattering defeat "the black day of the German Army."

The two Allied triumphs of July and August convinced Foch, who had just been elevated to marshal, that the war had entered a new stage. Before, his idea had been to straighten out the line and keep the enemy off balance until the Allies were ready to go over to the offensive—probably in the spring of 1919. Now he realized that the decisive campaign might be started before winter weather set in. Swiftly he began preparations for an all-out offensive aimed at the center of the German line in the Meuse-Argonne region.

Meanwhile Pershing was well advanced in his long-delayed plans to create an American army and assemble it for independent operations against the Saint-Mihiel salient, the last such German-held pocket in the Allied line. Then on August 30, the very day that Pershing took official command of the Saint-Mihiel front, Foch arrived and told him abruptly of his new plan, which would limit the Saint-Mihiel operation and use American divisions as part of French armies in the Meuse-Argonne.

Pershing, too, sensed that the pace of events was quickening, but he could not and would not tolerate the dispersal of his forces. Foch snapped, "Do you wish to take part in the battle?" Pershing declared, "If you will assign me a sector I will take it at once." As the meeting reached its climax, Foch insisted that Pershing accept the new project. Both men rose angrily to their feet. "Marshal Foch," Pershing declared, "you may insist all you please, but I decline absolutely to agree to your plan. While our army will fight wherever you may decide, it will not fight except as an independent American army."

In fact, Pershing was willing to fight in the big new offensive, but not before

One day in 1917 Billy Mitchell's car broke down on a French road. An escorting automobile stopped and its chauffeur quickly repaired Mitchell's car. Mitchell, impressed by the young man, asked his name. "Eddie, sir," was the reply. It was Eddie Rickenbacker (above), who was to become the greatest U.S. ace.

his fledgling army had been tested, as an army, in the easier undertaking at Saint-Mihiel, which the Germans had held tranquilly since 1914 and which was now manned by second-line troops. The two leaders finally reached a compromise. Foch promised to supply Pershing with artillery, tank and air support, and Pershing in return contracted to move his army to the Meuse-Argonne front as soon as it had attained its initial objectives at Saint-Mihiel.

Pershing admitted this double-barreled commitment was "a gigantic task." He said, "Plans for this second concentration involved the movement of some 600,000 men and 2,700 guns, more than half of which would have to be transferred from the battlefield of Saint-Mihiel by only three roads, almost entirely during the hours of darkness. In other words, we had undertaken to launch with practically the same army, within the next twenty-four days, two great attacks on battlefields sixty miles apart." But the tremendous facilities of his Services of Supply and the brilliant staff work of Colonel George Marshall would put the troops and matériel into action right on schedule.

The attack on the Saint-Mihiel salient began in the early hours of September 12 with a heavy bombardment. Overhead, about 800 planes were spotting for the artillery, strafing and dropping bombs. All of these planes were of British and French manufacture, but most of the fliers were Americans. Before 1917, a band of reckless youths from the United States had joined the French air service. Developing into first-rate pilots, they won fame as the Lafayette Escadrille and inherited the reputation for romantic gallantry enjoyed by the cavalry in previous wars. When America declared war, most of them transferred to form the nucleus of the United States Air Service. They were joined by hundreds of other youngsters, many of whom started their training at Kelly Field in Texas. The Air Service had scores of well-publicized heroes, including Raoul Lufberry, Jim McConnell, James Norman Hall (later a novelist and co-author of *Mutiny on the Bounty*) and Eddie Rickenbacker, an ex-automobile racer who eventually shot down 21 enemy planes. Colonel (later General) Billy Mitchell presided over this flamboyant force, preaching the gospel he had learned from the English General Hugh Trenchard—that massed air power was capable of destroying the enemy's will and capacity to resist. Except for observation work, the air forces in World War I were more colorful than effective, but the sorties over Saint-Mihiel represented the greatest display of air power up to that point.

AFTER this heavy bombardment by ground and air, Pershing at 5 a.m. unleashed the half-million men of the American First Army. It was a walkover. The strategic burden of the attack was carried by the 1st and the 26th Divisions, both of them now hardened veterans. The 1st pierced the eastern face of the salient, the 26th drove in from the western face. Just 24 hours after the assault had begun, these two divisions linked up in the rain near the flaming town of Vigneulles, sealing off the rest of the salient to the south. As the other divisions advanced along the perimeter of the salient, the town of Saint-Mihiel quickly fell and many defenders elsewhere surrendered at their first chance. The entire attack ended just four days later with fewer casualties than the 1st Division alone had suffered at Soissons. Pershing felt that the victory gave his troops the added confidence they needed. He thought it gave encouragement to "the tired Allies." Above all, he believed that it "completely demonstrated the wisdom of building up a distinct American army."

General Billy Mitchell, the foresighted exponent of air power, insisted that all orders he issued be clear enough to avoid costly mistakes. To ensure this, he read each order to a valued officer who was "not particularly bright." If this aide could understand the order, Mitchell was sure anyone could.

Alvin York was extremely modest about his stupendous exploit in the Argonne Forest. When he reported to his brigade commander to deliver his prisoners, the general said, "Well, York, I hear you have captured the whole damned German army." York replied, "I only have one hundred and thirty-two."

The aggressive Marine above was sketched by John W. Thomason Jr., artist, author and a career officer in the Marine Corps. Thomason, a drawling, deadpan Texan who spent much of his boyhood listening to aging Confederate veterans reminiscing, was awarded the Navy Cross and the Silver Star for attacking a machine-gun position and killing 13 Germans.

As soon as victory was assured, American divisions began hiking to assembly areas and shuttling in precisely timed truck and rail convoys to the Meuse-Argonne front 60 miles west. September 26 was the day when the great new offensive was to begin. Some 200,000 Americans were to be on the starting line then (eventually more than one million took part). On the right of the new American front lay the Meuse. Wide and deep, the river followed a twisting course between formidable cliffs; from the 50- to 200-foot heights, German artillery looked down on the doughboys. On the Americans' left sprawled the Argonne Forest; its vast tangles of trees and thorny underbrush were honeycombed with tunnels and concrete dugouts which might disgorge at any moment a German flanking force. The front itself was 25 miles wide—a shell-torn wasteland studded with hills and cut with ravines that masked mortars, machine guns and riflemen. In the 500 square miles that lay ahead of the starting line, 117,000 Allied soldiers, over half of them Americans, would be killed or wounded before the Meuse-Argonne campaign came to its end.

On the night of September 25, some 4,000 field pieces blazed away at the German line. At dawn the American First Army, nine divisions strong, went over the top. Doughboys in their battered helmets and muddy puttees dashed forward. In the dense fog men strayed from their own platoons and companies, stumbled into bogs or shell holes. The enemy was blinded too, and the German forward positions were overrun, with few American casualties. But around 10 o'clock, when the sun began breaking through, German guns started to tear great holes in the long, ragged advancing line.

The primary goal of the attack was Montfaucon, a village on a height almost midway between the Meuse and the Argonne. This command post, from which the enemy could see as far as Verdun, 14 miles away, had to be taken if any gains were to be made and held. But the slopes on all sides were exposed to fire, and the Americans attacking from the front were pinned down a mile and a half away. Dusk came with Montfaucon still in the enemy's hands, and with German reinforcements and supplies moving briskly toward the front. Trench maps in Pershing's headquarters that night showed an offensive penetration of one to five miles, but the positions essential to continuing the advance were still out of grasp.

A LIGHT rain which had been falling sporadically for a week continued all night and on into the next day. Heavy traffic turned the shell-raked barrens into swamps in which artillery caissons and supply wagons sank to the hubs. (One artillery outfit bogged down in the mud near Montfaucon was under the command of a peppery young Missourian of the 35th Division, Captain Harry S. Truman.) Neither guns nor shells were moving forward. Doggedly the infantry divisions pressed ahead as far as they could. With the aid of a few French tanks, a National Guard unit from Baltimore succeeded in pushing up to Montfaucon. Hemmed in on three sides, the enemy pulled out. The crucial height of Montfaucon became American. But the whole advance during the first week carried no more than six miles.

By now troops from Saint-Mihiel were arriving in force. Pershing pulled out tired, battle-thinned units and put in his veteran divisions. Plans were drawn up for another offensive surge, to open on October 4. Its objective was to breach the Hindenburg line, a deep, intricate network of trenches and dugouts which protected some 250 miles of the German front.

While this move was in preparation, accidental immortality came to a unit of the 77th Division. This New York division, whose commanding general characterized it as "a group of hardy frontiersmen from the Bowery and the Lower East Side," began moving up along the edge of the Argonne Forest. Suddenly one of its battalions lost contact with headquarters. The battalion commander, Major Charles W. Whittlesey, sent runners back and discovered that the Germans were on all sides. Instead of surrendering, he and his men dug in and kept fighting. Although their rations were gone and their position under bombardment by both German and Allied artillery, they still held out. One message from the "lost battalion" was delivered to the division's command post by a wounded, one-eyed carrier pigeon. The note read, "We are along the road parallel 276.4. Our own artillery is dropping a barrage directly on us. For heaven's sake, stop it." At last, after five days, their division rescued them. Of the battalion's original 600 men, less than half survived.

THE new American attack started on schedule, but despite ferocious effort it got almost nowhere. Except on the edge of the Argonne, where the redoubtable 1st Division was in action, reports to A.E.F. headquarters seldom told of gains greater than a few hundred yards. This seemed pitifully little compared with the steady gains that the British were making along the Belgian border. Impatiently Pershing began relieving officers and berating his staff. He formed a Second Army out of the divisions still around Saint-Mihiel, appointed General Robert Bullard as its commander and put General Hunter Liggett in charge of the First Army. Earlier he had distrusted Liggett, feeling that a man so fat was probably lazy and slow, but Liggett had proved his own assertion that he had no fat above the neck. Pershing sent one corps commander back to a division, replacing him with General Summerall, and ordered countless majors and colonels off to Blois, a reassignment center which he used as a dump for the incompetent and the inefficient. In Paris there were mutterings that Pershing was the one who ought to be relieved; a suggestion to this effect got as far as Marshal Foch, who promptly scotched it. Few military men realized then what has since been generally conceded—that the Meuse-Argonne area was the toughest terrain of the front.

There were redeeming moments. During the October 4 offensive, a patrol from the 82nd Division was trapped and almost massacred just east of the Argonne. One of the survivors was a tall, red-haired mountaineer from Tennessee, Corporal Alvin C. York. A conscientious objector at the beginning of the war, he intended to obey the Biblical injunction against killing. Unfortunately for the Germans, an army captain had argued him out of his conviction. When an enemy platoon charged down on him, he shot 25 and ultimately returned with more than 100 captives. Foch called this feat "the greatest thing accomplished by any private soldier in all the armies of Europe." York and other heroes offered some relief from the mounting lists of men killed in action.

Still the offensive made little headway. Through all of October the new ground won amounted to less than that taken in the first attack of September 26. The wounded, together with victims of a raging influenza epidemic, poured in so fast that the medical corps had to borrow 45 hospital trains from the French; the ambulance drivers and field nurses worked around the clock.

But by now Ludendorff had told the civilian leaders in Berlin of the conviction he had held since summer—that the nation was beaten. Desperate feel-

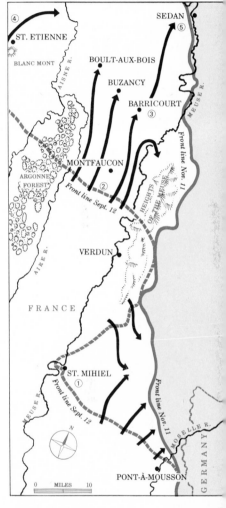

YANKS AT SAINT-MIHIEL
AND THE MEUSE-ARGONNE

On September 12, 1918, seven American divisions took the lead in smashing the German-held Saint-Mihiel salient (1). Two weeks later nine U.S. divisions launched a massive offensive against the 25-mile-long front (2) between the Argonne Forest and Meuse River. The first U.S. objective, Montfaucon, was seized the next day, but slowed down by the rugged terrain, they did not capture Barricourt (3) until November 1. By taking Boult-aux-Bois, they enabled the French on their left (4) to cross the Aisne. The Yanks were in the hills near Sedan (5) when the war ended.

ers for an armistice had gone out from Germany, and the troops, catching a scent of what was in the air, had begun to lay down their arms and desert. Germany's allies collapsed. Bulgaria, then Turkey, then Austria-Hungary capitulated. By the end of October the weakening of morale, coupled with losses in battle had whittled some crack German divisions down to a few thousand shambling survivors. The enemy's lines began to crumble.

In the first week of November, Pershing's army found itself plunging forward. Exhilarated, Pershing ordered an attempt to take Sedan, which, as a symbol of the humiliation that France had suffered in 1870, might more tactfully have been left to the French. Pershing's mistake was only one of many. In the excitement and confusion, Colonel George Marshall passed on a directive telling commanders that they need not respect divisional boundaries. As a result the 1st Division veered haphazardly into the paths of the 42nd and 77th Divisions. At one point doughboys of the 1st "captured" the 42nd's commander, Brigadier General Douglas MacArthur. More than once Americans were on the point of killing Americans, and if they had entered Sedan they might have ended up fighting the French. But Pershing's good sense reasserted itself. He called off the Sedan operation and let the French take the city.

Two days later, on November 9, rumors of peace spread through ranks, touching off premature armistice celebrations. "But, now it is the *11th of November!*" wrote an A.E.F. veteran. "The real Armistice Day! Paris is soggy with rain. Paris is mad, utterly mad with joy. . . . Girls spring upon the running boards of motor cars moving slowly through the throngs; sometimes they

THE CENTRAL POWERS AT
HIGH TIDE IN EUROPE

This map shows the far-flung conquests of the Central Powers on four fronts in World War I. The early German onslaught in the west (1) almost engulfed Paris. In the east German armies hastened Russia's withdrawal from occupied territory up to the line (2) and later to dotted line (3). In Italy, Austria and Germany drove to the Piave (4), and they joined Bulgaria in the Balkans to crush Serbia (5) and invade Albania and Greece. But Germany, bled white by late 1918, could not hold the Western Front against the Allies with their mounting U.S. strength.

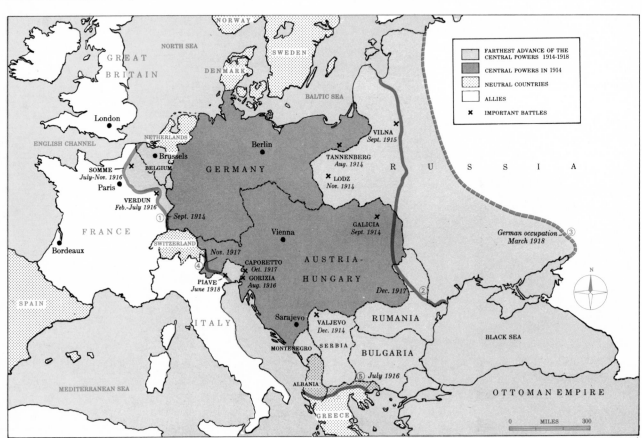

clamber over the sides, shouting convulsively. . . ." Along the front doughboys set bonfires and shot off rockets. Artillery Captain Alden Brooks reported, "At lunch we opened wine and quaffed each other's health and discussed future plans. . . . The war was over. Enough of this now. How much longer were we going to be kept hanging about in this wilderness?" To Father Francis P. Duffy, a chaplain with the 42nd Division, the war's end brought thoughts of American casualties (112,000 dead and 237,000 wounded), and he wrote that "All day I had a lonely and an aching heart." And on November 12 outside Paris, Marshal Foch, who had done as much as any single man to win the war, was visited by General John J. Pershing, whose fresh young manpower had finally turned the tide. Their quarrels were forgiven in the full flush of success. Pershing wrote: "What was said and the realization that the victory was won and the war actually over affected us both deeply and for some moments we were speechless. Both of us were rather overcome by emotion as we embraced and each gave the other the time-honored French 'accolade.'"

In September 1918 the flu epidemic reached frightening proportions, evoking macabre humor: "I had a little bird named 'Enza,' I opened the window and in-flu-enza." But it was no joke. In 10 months a half million died in the U.S.; flu and pneumonia killed half as many troops at home as died in battle. The policeman above is wearing a mask to avoid contamination.

T HROUGHOUT the anguished days of battle, President Wilson had kept the day of peace uppermost in his mind. He had largely delegated to others the job of running the war effort at home; he had given Pershing virtually a free hand in France; but he retained in his own hands the task of concluding the peace settlement.

In 1917 the Allies had told him something of their secret treaties under which Italy was promised territory in return for entering the war and Britain and France would receive postwar spheres of influence in the Middle East. Wilson paid little attention, but he did write to Colonel Edward House, his close friend and adviser, that he felt that "England and France *have not the same views with regard to peace that we have by any means.*"

In a message to Congress on January 8, 1918, Wilson explained his conception of what a peace treaty should contain if it was to end the threat of future wars. He outlined 14 points, most of them dealing with such specific problems as the indemnification of Belgium and the restoration of Alsace-Lorraine to France. He endorsed the principle of self-determination by nationality groups—in Poland, in the polyglot Austro-Hungarian Empire and in the Turkish Empire. He advocated that diplomacy be open, arms reduced to the lowest possible levels, trade barriers destroyed, the seas opened to every people, and above all that a "general association of nations . . . be formed . . . for the purpose of affording mutual guarantees of political independence and territorial integrity to great and small states alike."

Later, in 1918, Wilson reiterated and amplified these points, stressing his desire for a peace "just to victors and vanquished alike." The nobility, generosity and idealism of his language made a profound impression on people everywhere who hoped that a better world might emerge from the war. When the Germans at last realized that all was lost, they appealed to Wilson for an armistice and a peace based on his Fourteen Points and other declarations.

Sent through Swiss channels, the first message from Berlin reached Wilson on October 7. The British and the French had already learned of the appeal and had condemned it as a German ruse to split the alliance. Numerous Americans had the same suspicion and demanded that Germany be utterly crushed before peace was made. Wilson thought differently. Suspecting that the Germans might be at the end of their rope, he entered into correspondence with

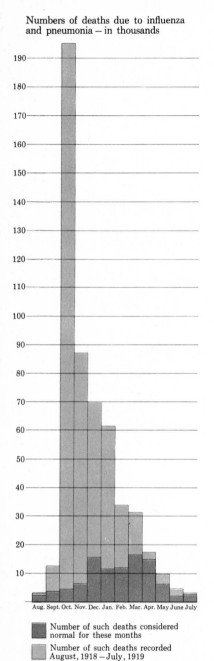

Numbers of deaths due to influenza
and pneumonia — in thousands

190
180
170
160
150
140
130
120
110
100
90
80
70
60
50
40
30
20
10

Aug. Sept. Oct. Nov. Dec. Jan. Feb. Mar. Apr. May June July

Number of such deaths considered
normal for these months

Number of such deaths recorded
August, 1918 – July, 1919

PROFILE OF THE FLU

EPIDEMIC, 1918-1919

*This graph shows the monthly
death rate due to influenza and
related diseases during the epidemic of 1918-1919, as compared
with the non-epidemic year, 1915
(lower part of each bar). In October 1918 the epidemic reached its
peak, taking 193,865 lives. Before
the epidemic ended in July 1919,
about 20 million Americans sick-
ened and more than 500,000 died.*

them, raising in each communication one or more additional issues: Would
the German government agree in advance to abide by his points and principles, not merely to negotiate about them? Would it demonstrate good faith by
halting submarine operations? Would it democratize its government? Would
it let the Allies decide upon the military conditions necessary to prevent a re-
sumption of hostilities? To each, the Germans responded in the affirmative.

Meanwhile, Colonel House went off to Paris. Meeting with the British,
French and Italian prime ministers, he asked whether they, too, would agree
to be bound by Wilson's principles. When they expressed reservations, the
colonel remarked that the President might conceivably have to go before Congress, say that the Allies were not fighting for the same objectives as the
United States, and raise the question of a separate peace. Faced with this
ultimatum, the premiers began to concede that they did subscribe to almost
all of what Wilson had said. An agreement was reached stipulating that Wilson's principles should, in general, guide the drafting of a final peace treaty.

While the talks in Paris went on, Germany's collapse began. Mutiny broke
out in the fleet. Communist uprisings occurred. The kaiser abdicated and fled
to Holland. Picking up the pieces, Socialists proclaimed a republic. Delegates
had left for Compiègne, France, under a flag of truce. There, in a railroad car
on a siding at 5:30 a.m. on November 11, 1918, they signed a document which,
though termed an armistice, was equivalent to surrender.

AFTERWARD, there were to be bitter disputes between Americans, Englishmen and Frenchmen about whether the United States had "won the war"
or merely delivered a final blow. Many harsh things were said in Europe about
the performance of Americans in the Meuse-Argonne; many foolish things
were said by Americans about their former allies. Actually American soldiers
had performed as well as could be expected—no worse and no better than
English or French soldiers of comparable condition and experience. But without the presence of the two million Americans in France in 1918, the German
armies probably would not have been defeated. Without the foodstuffs, munitions, money and other essentials that the American economy supplied, the
Allies almost certainly would not have held out so long as they did. On the
other hand, the tally of dead and wounded—6,161,000 French, 3,190,000 British, 7,143,000 Germans, 349,000 Americans—proved that the worst of the war
had been waged before America joined in. There was no clear answer to the
question of whether the Allies or the United States deserved the greater credit. Furthermore, events would soon show that no one had won World War I.

Just a few days before the armistice, congressional elections had been held.
Wilson had asked the people to vote for Democrats, and he warned that failure
to do so would amount to repudiation of his leadership. The voters had nevertheless given both the House and Senate to the Republicans. Then came the
wild celebrations of the "false armistice," reported from Brest on November 7,
and the real armistice four days later. Crowds jammed city streets, kissing
and shouting. But almost at once they turned to other matters—the epidemic
of "Spanish flu," sweeping the country, the problem of high prices and the
worry of whether there would be enough jobs to go around once the soldiers
came home.

Wilson came to Europe in December 1918 to sit at the peace table and
ensure that his principles actually were written into the final treaty. He may

have convinced himself that he reflected the hopes and dreams of humanity at large, especially after the tumultuous welcome he had received in his preconference tour of Europe. Speaking to the French senate, Wilson said that he represented a nation whose heart was committed to making the right kind of peace and that he spoke for the people whom he represented. But in truth he did not. The seeds of his ultimate defeat had been firmly planted.

IT is understandable if the men facing Wilson across the conference table did not realize the weakness of the President's position. The other American commissioners were his hand-picked men: House, his closest friend; Secretary of State Robert Lansing; General Tasker H. Bliss, a former chief of staff; and Henry White, nominally a Republican, but accustomed, as a career diplomat, to doing what he was told. The legion of experts in the American delegation, like the commissioners, were almost all devoted to Wilson. Within a few months a good deal of this devotion would disappear.

For undisclosed reasons, House would suddenly lose his friend's confidence. Some of the younger and more idealistic experts like William C. Bullitt would become disillusioned and resign. Bullitt lost his faith when his attempts at reaching an agreement with the Bolsheviks were disregarded. Under pressure from the Allies in 1918, Wilson had reluctantly assigned units to take part in expeditions to northern Russia and Siberia. Although Wilson had ordered that there be no meddling in Russia's internal affairs, in effect the Americans were supporting anti-Bolshevik forces in Russia's civil war; American troops themselves had only one brief and accidental skirmish with the Bolsheviks. Bullitt came back from an unofficial mission to Moscow early in 1919 with proposals from Lenin that promised peace in the East and possible Russian participation in a postwar settlement. When Wilson ignored these and allowed Allied intervention to go on, Bullitt angrily left Paris. So did young Samuel Eliot Morison, who would later become an outstanding American historian, and Adolf A. Berle Jr., a precocious and brilliant lawyer who would be an adviser to both Franklin D. Roosevelt and John F. Kennedy. But none of these Americans in Paris were representatives of anyone but the President. While Europeans might know of the congressional elections and other indications of dissent, they heard only Wilson's voice. For them, he was America.

In the same sense, the men opposite him were their countries. David Lloyd George, the British prime minister, came to Paris only after calling a general election, the results of which guaranteed his coalition cabinet a majority in the House of Commons. Lloyd George had traveled a sinuous path to power. Early in the century he had been opposed to British imperialism; by 1911 he had switched to advocacy of naval preparedness. A leader of the Liberal left, he made common cause during the war with the Tories, became premier with their aid and championed vengeful war—no compromise, no negotiated peace, nothing but a "knockout blow." "We shall squeeze the German orange until the pips squeak," one of his followers had said. Lloyd George, with a mind that moved twice as fast as other men's and a conscience that, as he said, he kept "well under control," was not prepared to accept any treaty that would not satisfy the British electorate.

Neither was Clemenceau of France prepared to make concessions that might be unpopular in his country. At 78, he was no longer thinking so much of his own career; he believed that the French people had suffered more than the

These snowbound soldiers were among the 5,000 Americans sent to Archangel in the chaotic period after Russia left the war. The troops never understood the purpose of their mission. The armistice found them stuck in Russia —confused, homesick, fending off Bolshevik raiders. After suffering some 400 casualties, the Americans were withdrawn in July 1919.

English or Americans, that they had earned the right to taste revenge, that they deserved security for the future. If these goals required harsh peace terms and violation of the Fourteen Points, too bad.

As the representative of the host nation, Clemenceau presided at meetings of the heads of delegations. Gray gloves masked the eczema on his hands. Sitting stolidly, he often closed his heavy eyelids in real or feigned sleep. His inner force became apparent only when he lashed out in some curt, usually epigrammatic statement cutting to the marrow of an issue. "God gave us His Ten Commandments, and we broke them," he reportedly said: "Wilson gave us his Fourteen Points—we shall see."

Edward M. House, Wilson's closest friend and trusted adviser, disliked the title "Colonel" that had been bestowed upon him in the 1890s by James Hogg, governor of Texas. To go with the title, Hogg gave him a luxurious full-dress uniform, which House presented to his coachman. The coachman immediately rose to become the supreme grand master of his lodge.

THE other plenipotentiaries were less powerful personalities. Vittorio Orlando and Sidney Sonnino were eloquent pleaders for Italy. They had promised their country satisfaction, and they meant to bring home the territories in the Alps promised them in the secret treaties. They also meant to have Fiume, which had been promised them by no one. The Japanese, Baron Makino and Viscount Chinda, wanted title to the former German leaseholds in China as well as German island possessions in the Pacific. They could sit impassively, outwaiting Wilson and everyone else, for their troops were already in possession and were going to be hard to dislodge. The premiers of the British dominions, especially Jan Christian Smuts for the Union of South Africa and William H. Hughes for Australia, had their designs on other former German colonies. Once when Wilson asked in a solemn tone if Australia would defy the opinion of all the civilized world, Hughes, with a straight face, answered, "That's about the size of it, President Wilson."

In addition, there were competing delegations from the new states that had risen on the ruins of the Austro-Hungarian and Turkish Empires. There were also spokesmen for causes, ranging from temperance to the outlawry of vivisection. Functionaries circled importantly from the Hotel Crillon, where Wilson had his headquarters, to the Hotel Majestic, center of the British delegation, to makeshift offices all over Paris, to the monumental buildings on the Quai d'Orsay where the meetings were held. All this took place between January and July 1919, when Paris was still euphoric about peace and the streets were filled with rioting soldiers demanding demobilization. Sir Harold Nicolson, then a young expert in the British delegation, said that the whole atmosphere was that of "a riot in a parrot house."

Dealing with such determined and adroit men as Lloyd George and Clemenceau, Wilson found that the pre-conference agreement on the Fourteen Points was dissolving. On the way over he had said to his experts, "Tell me what is right and I'll fight for it." But the issues often proved too complicated for simple judgments of right and wrong. Wilson found himself poring over maps that showed overlapping lingual, cultural and historical frontiers. Even where these coincided, there was usually some soldier or economist to say that they did not make sense from a military or economic point of view. Wilson had always concentrated on one question at a time, mastered it, dealt with it and moved on to another—all on his own. In Paris, however, no one man could comprehend all the issues. Efforts by Wilson to do so led to exhaustion, exhaustion to impatience, and impatience to concession.

Wilson had decided that the creation of a League of Nations was the first and most important task. He succeeded in getting a League Covenant drafted before any other major questions were settled. But after it had been accepted, Wilson learned that he would have to make changes. A round-robin resolution had been circulated in Washington by Senator Henry Cabot Lodge on March 3, 1919, and signed by more than a third of the Senate. It stated quite bluntly that the proposed League of Nations was unacceptable. To win ratification Wilson would have to secure amendments safeguarding the Monroe Doctrine, confirming the rights of each nation to set tariffs and immigration quotas and permitting resignation from the League. The Allies made Wilson pay a high price for their acceptance of these amendments.

He gave ground stubbornly. Another man might have intimidated the hungry, exhausted Allies, fearful of the threat of revolution, with the strong economic weapons Wilson possessed. He preferred to win by debate. At one point, however, when the victors became adamant in their opposition, Wilson ordered his ship made ready for return to the United States. The threat worked. In the end he could count some triumphs. Instead of simply being turned over to the Allies the German Saar and the Rhineland were to be occupied temporarily; ultimately the Rhineland would be restored to Germany; the Saar's fate would be determined by a plebiscite. Boundaries for the new nations in Central Europe and for the Balkan States were drawn with at least some regard for ethnic and lingual divisions and the apparent wishes of the population. Though Orlando and Sonnino walked out and swore they would not sign the treaty, Wilson refused to give Italy Fiume, a city surrounded by a Slav population and the only good port available to Yugoslavia.

A German delegation was summoned to the Versailles Palace in May and given a month in which to examine the terms. Then, their protests all but disregarded, they were compelled to sign a document depriving Germany of six million people, stripping it of armaments, making inevitable a plunge into bankruptcy, and declaring that Germany bore the complete guilt for the war and its devastation. The echoes of Wilson's inspiring orations were few and far between in the treaties signed with the Germans and the other members of the defeated Central Powers.

Wilson was forced by the Allies to compromise his plan for peace— the Fourteen Points. Besides demanding onerous reparations and the humiliation of Germany, the peace negotiators violated the spirit of the First Point by barring newsmen from most of their sessions. A sarcastic cartoon (above) flayed this affront to "open covenants of peace, openly arrived at."

EVEN before it was signed, the Versailles pact was being damned. The editors of the *New Republic*—Herbert Croly, who had been the philosopher of Roosevelt's Bull Moose movement; Walter Weyl, another prophet of progressivism; and 30-year-old Walter Lippmann—proclaimed their refusal to endorse a document that "merely . . . [wrote] the specifications for future revolutions and war." In *The Economic Consequences of the Peace*, published in 1920, English economist John Maynard Keynes wrote that the peace, "if it is carried into effect, must impair yet further, when it might have restored, the delicate, complicated organization, already shaken and broken by war, through which alone the European peoples can employ themselves and live."

On the return trip to America, a tired and exasperated Wilson conceded that the treaty had flaws. But, he said, it also contained the Covenant of the League of Nations. And the League, by deliberative processes, could in time repair whatever was wrong. Above all, it could guarantee mankind against any repetition of the horrors which had just passed. "Unless America takes part in this treaty," he would predict, ". . . the world is going to lose heart." America was, said Wilson, "the Nation upon which the whole world depended to hold the scales of justice even. If we fail them, God help the world!"

URGING TEMPERANCE, this horse-drawn group of children and adults, supporters of the Woman's Christian Temperance Union, parades its slogans around 1915. Founded in 1874, the organization also made strenuous efforts for prison reform, women's suffrage and the prohibition of tobacco and of child labor.

A noble effort to keep America dry

THE passage of the 18th Amendment, which prohibited the manufacture, sale or transportation of intoxicating liquors, marked the last victory of the defenders of a simpler past over what Walter Lippmann called "the new urban civilization, with its irresistible scientific and economic mass power." In this sense, prohibition was not only a protest against "Demon Rum"; it was also a defense of the old rural America against the threat of industrialism and social change.

From earliest colonial times, farmers and frontiersmen had viewed the cities as strongholds of Satan, seedbeds of every sort of real and imagined vice from atheism to alcoholism. In the 19th Century the Woman's Christian Temperance Union and the Anti-Saloon League enlisted adherents who saw these reform groups as inspired defenders of a sober, agrarian way of life. (Although drinking was prevalent in rural areas, it was seldom acknowledged as a problem.) During World War I the consumption of alcohol was at times equated with treason, for many brewers were of German origin and brewing used up enough barley each day to have made 11 million loaves of bread for the soldiers. By 1919 the "drys" had secured the ratification of the amendment. "Goodbye John [Barleycorn]," said the revivalist preacher Billy Sunday. "You were God's worst enemy. You were Hell's best friend. . . . The reign of tears is over." The reign of highly organized crime, however, had just begun.

INGENIOUS CONCEALMENT of liquor—strapped to the leg, hidden in waistbands, poured into a hollow cane and tied to a belt—is seen in this painting. Before prohibition, bootleggers were simply those who hid whisky in their bootlegs. But from 1920 to 1933 the term covered everyone dealing in illegal alcohol—a traffic which exceeded 70 million gallons each year.

The route of illegal liquor

The blissful, bone-dry utopia which the prohibitionists foresaw failed to arrive. Instead, there flourished "a horde of bootleggers, moonshiners . . . racketeers . . . venal judges, corrupt police . . . crooked politicians . . ." Working together, this unholy brood took in billions of dollars selling their "hooch"

to an eager, thirsty public. Most of the liquor was manufactured surreptitiously at illegal stills; the steps in the distillery process are charted in the inset below. The rest of the whisky —$40 million worth in 1924 alone—was smuggled in from Canada and the Caribbean islands. This painting traces the travels of a shipment of liquor from a graceful rumrunner to the sprawling drunk who sampled it to excess. Presiding over the scene is the king of the liquor racket, Al "Scarface" Capone. On a wall is a temperance poster, an ironic reminder of the futility of an experiment Herbert Hoover called "noble in motive."

IRON GRILLEWORK DOOR, frequently the hallmark of speak-easies, is posted by a harassed New York City homeowner in an effort to dissuade drinkers from ringing the bell at all hours.

Bringing respectability
to sordid saloons

THANKS to prohibition, drinking became, according to economist Thorstein Veblen, a sign "of the superior status of those who are able to afford the indulgence." Heavy drinking, especially among women who previously would never have ventured into a saloon, was a badge of emancipation. To accommodate the drinkers, there were by 1933 some 219,000 illegal saloons called speakeasies. In plush, big-city "speaks," owner-hostesses like Texas Guinan, Belle Livingston and Helen Morgan cleared up to $4,000 a week for providing customers with exotic settings, songs and skits and Scotch at $25 per fifth. By contrast, there were the "smoke joints," where wood alcohol and Jamaica ginger blinded, paralyzed or killed thousands by the end of the era.

Twenty One West Fifty Second Street

VOLUNTEER 8756-8762

NEW STORK CLUB
51½ EAST 51⅜

No 4265   1933

Sherman Billingsley

MU-2-8221
EL-5-9003

MEMBERSHIP CARDS, open-sesames for two speakeasies (later transformed into headquarters for cafe society), bear only a number. Names were registered, but often kept secret.

A DRINKING SCENE, similar to those which took place in many of New York's speakeasies, shows rich revelers formally dressed. At Belle Livingston's place customers were required

WRECKED INTERIOR shows the violence with which this speakeasy was raided. But gaining a conviction against its owner was harder. Bribed officials and corruptible federal agents made strict enforcement of the Volstead Act a virtual impossibility.

to sit on the floor in Oriental style because, as the proprietor said, "A man could get hurt falling off a bar stool." Helen Morgan entertained by singing blues and torch songs. When she was put on trial after a raid, her case was quickly dismissed by the jury, one of whose members argued, "We couldn't take the word of two prohibition agents against Miss Morgan."

The many ruses of "the two dry clowns"

FIFTEEN hundred hard-pressed prohibition agents were scarcely adequate to prevent 125 million people from manufacturing and consuming alcohol. It was "like trying to dry up the Atlantic with a post office blotter." Two agents, however, made a memorable attempt.

In 1920 Izzy Einstein was a postal clerk, 40 years old, 5 feet 5 inches tall. He weighed 225 pounds and was a local cutup on New York's Lower East Side. His friend Moe Smith was a few inches taller, a few pounds heavier and equally as witty. When Izzy first applied for the job, he was told that he didn't "look much like a detective." He didn't. Neither did Moe. But together this congenial pair worried bootleggers and speakeasy owners from coast to coast. During the next five years, to the constant amusement of the nation, Izzy and Moe, employing a variety of bizarre disguises, confiscated five million bottles of liquor worth $15 million and made more than 4,000 arrests. When, in 1925, they were eased out of their jobs "for the good of the service," the New York *Herald Tribune* editorialized: "They never made prohibition much more of a joke than it has been made by some of the serious-minded prohibition officers."

INSPECTING A STILL, Izzy and Moe are shown after a raid in New Orleans. Izzy was able to buy a drink 35 seconds after arriving. It took him 11 minutes in Pittsburgh, 21 in Chicago.

AFTER A RAID, Izzy strikes a characteristic pose. When making an arrest, he said, "Dere's sad news."

LOOKING FOR WHISKEY, Izzy checks a crate in 1923. When Izzy met Albert Einstein, the great scientist told him that he had discovered stars in the sky for a living. The rotund agent, never at a loss, replied, "I'm a discoverer, too, only I discover in the basements."

IMAGINATIVE DISGUISES, like those seen in this photograph of Moe taken in 1949, range from the rich to the ragged. In the Bronx Izzy wore a football uniform to uncover a place catering to athletes. In Brooklyn he donned a frock coat and carried a lawbook to gain admittance to a speakeasy catering to judges. Once, he carried a violin and found a spot favored by musicians.

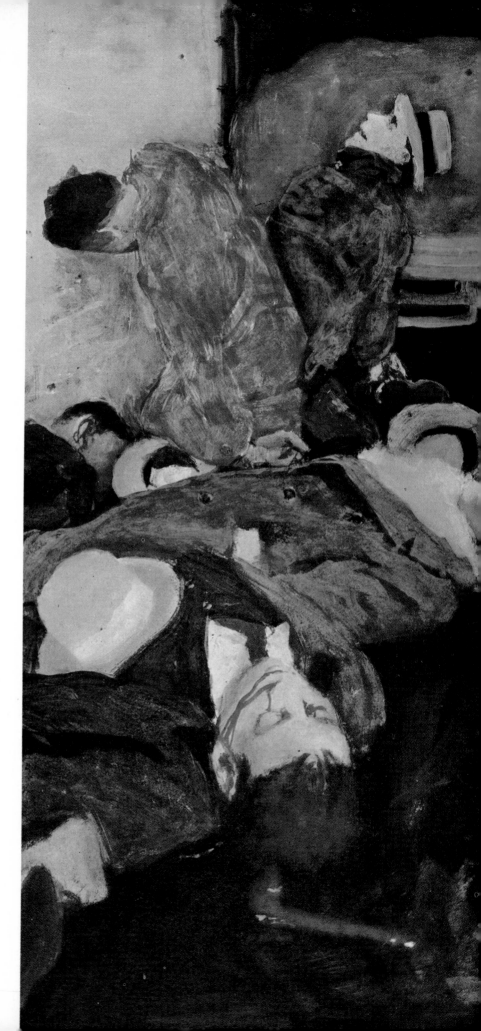

From gangster
to gangster:
a bloody valentine

"When I sell liquor," said an aggrieved Al Capone, "it's bootlegging. When my patrons serve it on a silver tray on Lake Shore Drive, it's hospitality." In 1927 Capone's ire should have been assuaged by his gang's revenue of some $60 million from bootlegging. When the competition tried to "muscle in," negotiations were usually conducted with submachine guns. In Chicago alone, there were 500 gangland murders between 1920 and 1930. The most spectacular, the Saint Valentine's Day massacre, is reconstructed in the painting at right. On February 14, 1929, five men, three in police uniforms, lined six members of Bugs Moran's gang, and a young optometrist unlucky enough to be present when the five came, against the wall of a garage. (Moran was Capone's biggest competitor.) It appeared to be a routine search, and the hoods were simply bored. Suddenly one of the plain-clothes men whipped out a machine gun and expertly sprayed his victims. The murders have never been solved.

3. RETURN
TO "NORMALCY"

IN February 1919, when Woodrow Wilson broke his stay in Paris with a brief trip home, he found the Senate was dividing into factions over the Versailles Treaty. By midsummer most Democrats were ready to vote for ratification. Nearly all Republicans, on the other hand, resented both their lack of real representation on the peace delegation and the political profit the Democrats would gain from ratification; a number had genuine misgivings about that section of the treaty that established the League of Nations. About a dozen Republicans, the "mild reservationists," believed the Senate should vote minor reservations or amendments in order to improve the treaty and make it represent bipartisan opinion. Another 20 or so wanted more important amendments, primarily to reduce American commitments; these were "strong reservationists." Finally, there were the "irreconcilables"—14 Republicans and one Democrat—those who were opposed to America's entering the League at all and were determined to defeat the treaty with or without reservations. This "Battalion of Death," as it was called, was led by the lion-maned Senator William E. Borah of Idaho, probably the greatest orator in the chamber, and included Philander Knox, who had been Taft's Secretary of State; Hiram W. Johnson, progressive leader in California and Theodore Roosevelt's running mate in 1912; Frank Brandegee of Connecticut; and the lone Democrat, James A. Reed of Missouri.

Both the strong reservationists and the irreconcilables knew that in July

GENIAL AND INEPT, President Warren G. Harding betrays neither trait in this magisterial portrait. He died in office as corrupt henchmen and cronies were being exposed.

The above cartoon from Britain's "Punch" casts a somewhat jaundiced eye on the infant League of Nations. The uneasy feeling about surrendering national sovereignty to an untried and possibly unwieldy organization was widespread. While the peace dove is willing to accept an olive branch from a solicitous President Wilson, she asks, "Isn't this a stick?"

1919 the large majority of the people wanted the United States in the League. Not many of these, however, had really fervent opinions. The minority that opposed the treaty did. German-Americans were angry about the treaty's harsh terms; Irish-Americans saw the League as a means of perpetuating their anathema, the British Empire; Italian-Americans, including Fiorello La Guardia in New York, resented Wilson's handling of the Fiume issue; others opposed giving Japan, over China's protest, ownership of the former German properties in Shantung; many progressives, both Democrats and Republicans, agreed with the editors of the *New Republic* that the treaty betrayed the ideals Wilson had voiced before and during the war. The irreconcilables expected that the fires of the opposition groups would burn a good deal longer than the feebler flame of the groups supporting the treaty. The obvious tactic, therefore, was to stall off a vote.

As chairman of the Foreign Relations Committee, Senator Henry Cabot Lodge could delay floor debate almost indefinitely. A slight, brusque man with irritating mannerisms, Lodge had a Ph.D. in political science from Harvard and he never forgave Wilson for taking over the title of the "scholar in politics." As political differences between the two men deepened, Lodge came to despise Wilson. Although Lodge said he wanted the treaty ratified with strong reservations, he behaved as though the outcome was less important to him than was the humiliation of the President.

Lodge was able to fill four Republican vacancies on his 17-man committee with strong reservationists and irreconcilables, thus increasing the strength of this bloc to six. When the treaty reached him, he insisted on taking two full weeks to read aloud all 268 pages of its text. Then for another six weeks of public hearings he summoned witness after witness, many of whom talked at length about wholly irrelevant matters and most of whom opposed ratification. Most of the newspaper reports of this testimony strengthened the emotions of those who were hostile to the treaty. Pittsburgh millionaires Henry Clay Frick and Andrew Mellon financed a massive propaganda campaign that encouraged hostility to the treaty. Meanwhile the majority of the people were losing interest in the issue.

Wilson had underestimated the strength of the opposition to the treaty and counted on much firmer support from the country. He was furious at the success of Lodge and the irreconcilables, and he decided to appeal to the country. If he could revive the enthusiasm of the majority, perhaps he could force ratification.

On September 3, 1919, Wilson set out from Washington on a special train to deliver some 40 speeches and a number of whistle-stop talks. He traveled through Ohio, across the Midwest, to Seattle, down into Hiram Johnson's home state and back through the Southwest. As he moved west the crowds grew larger and their cheers louder, and Wilson, as always, responded to his audience. On September 25 at Pueblo, Colorado, where he had intended only a short talk, the applause was such that he spoke for much longer than he had planned, orating with such feeling that tears appeared in the audience.

After this Pueblo speech, he complained of a headache. Unlike others that he had had since Paris, this one would not go away. He spent a sleepless night. His doctor found him seriously ill and ordered him to cancel the rest of the trip. Back in Washington, he attempted to rest and waited for the public to put pressure on the Senate. But on the morning of October 2 he told his wife that his left hand was numb. While she was calling the White House physician, she heard a noise from the bathroom. Wilson had collapsed on the floor, his left side from face to toe paralyzed by a stroke.

For three weeks Wilson was in bed, unable even to look at urgent messages. After that he slowly regained enough strength so that he could sometimes work for as much as an hour or two in a day. At these times, though his mind and memory were clear, he was querulous. He would break into tears. Never very tolerant of disagreement, now he could not stand it.

Mrs. Wilson appointed herself his unofficial guardian. A handsome, forceful woman who had married Wilson after the death of his first wife, she was devoted to him. Her main concern was to see that he suffered as few irritations and distractions as possible. "Woodrow Wilson," she explained later, "was first my beloved husband whose life I was trying to save . . . after that he was the President of the United States."

She agreed with Wilson's doctors who opposed his resigning, possibly because they feared the effect on his will to recover. She protected him against callers, censored the news that reached him and leafed through his mail in order to block anything that might upset him. As one historian has said, she was for all practical purposes "the first woman President of the United States." For the remainder of his term, Wilson was more often than not chief executive in little more than name.

One result was that when the treaty finally came before the whole Senate, pro-ratification forces were virtually leaderless. Gilbert M. Hitchcock of Nebraska, who had just become minority leader in the Senate, lacked experience, initiative and parliamentary skill. He looked to the White House for signals. Lodge's second report on the treaty recommended that it be approved subject to a number of reservations, most of which added up to the innocuous requirement that Congress should have a voice in any decision on action required under the Covenant.

Before his tour, Wilson had secretly drawn up a list of four reservations that he would accept, if necessary. If, during the committee hearings, Wilson had announced his willingness to accept these compromises, ratification might have been assured. By the time the ill President returned to Washington, the Senate debate had begun. Although it was clear that Lodge's position was much stronger, Hitchcock was told to make no concessions to Lodge. It was the President and not Mrs. Wilson who made this decision. She wanted the treaty issue resolved, no matter how, to ease her husband's mind, but he said to her, "Little girl, don't you desert me; that I cannot stand."

Henry Cabot Lodge, the archenemy of the League of Nations, cut an awesome figure in the Senate. His bearing was so dignified that he was once called the "ambassador from Massachusetts." His scholarship was just as impressive, though one wag declared that his mind was like the landscape of New England—"naturally barren, but highly cultivated."

ON November 19, 1919, all but four Democrats followed Hitchcock's lead and voted nay to the treaty with the Lodge reservations. Ironically, the irreconcilables joined the Administration forces and the vote was 55 against, 39 for. The Democrats then asked for a vote on the treaty without reservations. This time the irreconcilables formed a bloc with reservationists, and the count was 38 for, 53 against. In both versions the treaty was defeated.

No one could quite believe the decision was final. Through the succeeding winter, such believers in the League as ex-President Taft and ex-Secretary of State Elihu Root urged Republican reservationists to modify their demands. A number of Democrats, including William Jennings Bryan, pleaded with the

President for some kind of compromise. Wilson, however, remained stubborn. At one point he considered asking senators who voted against the treaty to resign and seek re-election, as they would have had to do under a parliamentary form of government. He talked and wrote of the approaching 1920 election as "a great and solemn referendum" on the League issue, and he seriously thought of running for a third term. When the treaty was again voted upon by the Senate, in March 1920, he stood by his earlier order. Once more it went down to defeat. Although the treaty was imperfect and may have contributed to the world's later troubles, the failure of the United States to join the world organization that Wilson had created was unquestionably a tragedy.

While opponents of the treaty gloated, Charles Evans Hughes, Elihu Root and others formed a committee of 31 to urge that the United States join the League, with certain reservations. From the Republican nominee, Warren G. Harding, they could get only a vague statement of approval for a somewhat different kind of world organization. Harding's seven-million-vote defeat of Democrat James M. Cox and his running mate, Franklin D. Roosevelt, who had championed the League, gave comfort to those who felt that the public wanted no part in that body or, indeed, in international affairs.

Harding's Secretary of State, Charles Evans Hughes, secured Senate approval of a peace treaty with Germany that gave the United States all the benefits of the Versailles pact with none of the responsibilities. To stop a naval arms race in the Pacific, Hughes then negotiated, and the Senate ratified, a treaty that called for a 10-year halt in building capital ships and set the ratio for these vessels in the American, British and Japanese navies at 5:5:3. Hughes also signed a four-power treaty providing for American-British-French-Japanese discussions in the event of any threat to peace in the Pacific area. This the Senate ratified but with reservations, saying it was not an alliance and that the United States assumed no obligation to use force.

I N 1924 Senator Borah succeeded Lodge as chairman of the Foreign Relations Committee. For the next 15 years the arch-isolationist Borah was either chairman or senior Republican member of this powerful body. Borah overshadowed Hughes's successor, former Senator Frank Kellogg, to such an extent that the press called Borah the "Minister of Foreign Affairs of the United States."

Though the United States was the richest and most powerful state in the world in the 1920s, most of its international policy seems almost lunatic in retrospect. It was owed about $10 billion by its former allies. They, in turn, had the right under the peace treaties to exact like reparation sums from the defeated nations. But in making its reparations payments, Germany nearly went bankrupt and suffered an inflation that made the mark worthless. The sensible solution was for the United States to write off some of the Allied debt if the Allies would reduce their reparations claims to a point at which payment was within the means of the defeated nations. Neither Harding nor his successors nor the Senate nor most of the public could appreciate this. President Calvin Coolidge commented laconically of the Allies, "They hired the money, didn't they?" The result was that, through Wall Street banks, American investors lent Germany funds to pay the Allies so that the Allies could pay the American government. In the end, when a depression set in, both the Germans and the Allies defaulted and the American investor lost.

Office of the Postmaster General
Washington, D.C.

May 15, 1918.

Hon. T. H. Patten,
    Postmaster,
        New York City.
My dear Mr. Patten:

    With this letter, the Post Office Department inaugurates a regular aeroplane mail service. In this important work of developing an advanced medium of postal transportation, I feel that the Post Office Department will have the fullest cooperation of the New York Post Office in making it a success.

    This letter will be dispatched under the first aeroplane postage stamp to be sold by the Department, and canceled and autographed by the President of the United States. Please deliver the envelope to Mr. Noah Tausigg, 111 Wall Street, New York City, who will arrange to have it sold at auction for the benefit of the Red Cross, and who will start the bidding at one thousand dollars.

        Sincerely yours,

        Postmaster General.

The premier performance of airmail in 1918 was not particularly impressive. The plane, carrying this historic letter with its Wilson-autographed stamp, refused to start; then somebody remembered to fill the gas tank. The plane took off, whereupon the pilot promptly got lost and landed in a cow pasture. The mail went on to New York via a reliable train.

As Winston Churchill was to remark later, Coolidge's summation had been "true but not exhaustive."

The corollary to Borah's influential position was that the United States shunned full-fledged commitments to promote world peace. However it did participate in one very dramatic move—the effort to outlaw war by treaty, the cause that Borah seemed to favor. This was the idea that had caught the imaginations of such enthusiasts as Raymond Robins, the wartime head of the American Red Cross mission in Russia; university professor James T. Shotwell; and Nicholas Murray Butler, president of Columbia University, who kept hoping to graduate to the presidency of the United States. Although they differed with one another, their common object was to abolish war by persuading nations to promise in writing never to resort to aggression. In 1927 this oddly assorted group suddenly found what seemed an unexpected opportunity to translate their vision into reality.

After talking with Shotwell in Paris, French Foreign Minister Aristide Briand sent a message to the United States saying France would be glad to join with America in mutually renouncing the use of war. From France's standpoint it would be, in effect, a neutrality pact that would strengthen French security. Recognizing this, Secretary of State Kellogg used sulphurous language in speaking of Butler and his friends. But the project could not be discarded because it had picked up so much momentum. Kellogg had to find some method, as Senator George Moses commented, "to get rid of the damn thing." The solution was to invite adherence to the treaty by the whole world. In the end, 60-odd nations signed this Kellogg-Briand Pact that pledged them not to use force against one another. Within a little more than a decade almost all of them would be at war, thus confirming the doubts of skeptics who had noted the absence of provisions for enforcement of the pact. The treaty would be remembered only as a monument to the naiveté of the 1920s.

With much less fanfare, there were other developments of great significance for the future. The conciliatory efforts of Coolidge's ambassador to Mexico, Dwight W. Morrow, and Herbert Hoover's promise of nonintervention in Latin American internal affairs planted the seeds of what would later flower as the Good Neighbor Policy of Franklin Roosevelt. Drastic reforms turned a spoils-ridden foreign service into a career corps that by the '30s would be ranked among the best in the world. Advocates of the Wilsonian dream of world co-operation set out to create a better-informed public. To this end they launched such organizations as the Council on Foreign Relations and the Foreign Policy Association and founded journals to publicize studies by scholars in these fields; they encouraged study and teaching in the fields of diplomatic history and international relations and helped to rear a generation which in its maturity proved to be more sophisticated and realistic than its predecessors. However, for most Americans, absorbed in the frivolous life of the '20s, American foreign relations seemed in recess.

So did domestic politics. During the war reform activities were minimal. Wilson was far too busy to press further for the New Freedom. But progressivism's successes had given new impetus to the demands for women's rights and prohibition. Carrie Chapman Catt, successor to Susan B. Anthony as head of the National American Woman Suffrage Association, continued to build her organization's strength at the precinct level, in the various

From the outset the Volstead Act of 1919 was an unpopular piece of legislation. It also inspired one of the most devastating cartoon characters to appear in American newspapers—Rollin Kirby's "Prohibition." In a sarcastic comment on U.S. bondage to a detested law, this lantern-jawed rapscallion is leading his disciples in a chorus of "My Country, 'Tis of Thee."

state capitals and in Washington. Leading the more militant Congressional Union for Woman Suffrage, Dr. Alice Paul made use of tactics she had learned among English suffragettes. Her women burned President Wilson in effigy, marched in picket lines and got themselves arrested. The suffragettes became so strong that within a year after the war ended, they could induce Congress to pass a women's suffrage amendment and then get state legislatures to ratify it. After August 1920 the Constitution forbade the federal government or any state to deny the vote to a citizen on account of sex.

Temperance advocates had worked with equal zeal and success. They had formed an Anti-Saloon League, which, under the leadership of Edwin Dinwiddie and then of Wayne B. Wheeler, became one of the most formidable pressure groups in the country. It enlisted a number of pastors, especially among the evangelical Protestants, who could mobilize their congregations to elect or defeat a candidate. From the same source the league raised large sums of money, some of which went into political contributions, some into propaganda; between 1909 and 1923 its publishing house printed more than 100 million pamphlets.

In their dedication to the cause, some prohibitionists were ruthless. Local league leaders like James Cannon Jr. of Virginia made no secret of their willingness to support a "man of small influence" against "an exceedingly able man" so long as he promised to vote right on the liquor issue. Other men in the Anti-Saloon League took pride in their ability to subordinate everything else to their single objective. One testified proudly he had had to lie, bribe and drink to put over prohibition in America. "I have told enough lies for 'the cause' to make Ananias ashamed of himself."

The league's leaders found the war a help, for it enabled them to win a halt to distilling in order to save grain for use as food. They then pressed Congress to pass an amendment outlawing the manufacture and sale of alcoholic beverages. Many congressmen voted for it against their own better judgment, and in some instances against their consciences. In a rear-guard action that it hoped might hamstring the amendment, Congress attached a requirement that ratification had to be completed in seven years. However, state legislatures, especially in the South and Midwest, raced to ratify; the process was completed in 13 months. After January 1920 permanent prohibition was a fact, a fact that would have startling consequences in the decade that followed.

As the '20s began, there was another so-called reform cause—the restriction of immigration—that still aroused enthusiasm. Ever since the beginning of the century, when Italians and Eastern Europeans began entering in large numbers, agitation had grown for some legislation to limit the influx. Arguing from scanty and unscientific data, men such as Madison Grant and Lothrop Stoddard contended that Latins and Slavs were inferior races and that America would suffer if it lost its predominantly Anglo-Saxon and Teutonic character. Labor unions had also argued for restricted immigration to reduce competition for jobs. In prewar years opponents of unrestricted immigration had persuaded Congress to enact a bill making passage of a literacy test a prerequisite for immigration. Wilson vetoed the bill, saying: "Those who come seeking opportunity are not to be admitted unless they have already had one of the chief opportunities they seek—the opportunity of education."

In wartime, with nationalistic feeling at a high pitch, restrictionists raised

Forty years after Belva Lockwood whizzed through Washington on her tricycle as a demonstration of feminist hardihood, a sturdy band of suffragettes (above) cast their first ballots. Nobody was really surprised when women turned out to be just as fickle as men. A wit in Congress observed that "politics make strange bedfellows. Especially since women got into 'em."

their sights and demanded the establishment of national or racial quotas. There was considerable support for this demand, for a large part of the public was fearful of a flood of refugees from postwar Europe. A literacy test was imposed over Wilson's veto; as soon as he was out of the White House, a severe quota system was voted by Congress. Successive amendments and revisions during the '20s created a rigidly restrictive set of immigration laws, but in fact the pioneering effort had been completed before the decade began. There were men who fought this trend—men like Alfred E. Smith, Fiorello La Guardia and Boston's colorfully corrupt James Michael Curley were campaigning for a fairer deal for Americans of Irish and Italian descent.

Suffragettes envisioned a fuller and more meaningful national life with woman as a coequal steersman at the political helm. Unfortunately their fervor often evoked gales of laughter (not always unsympathetic) from the cartoonists. The broom-wielding lady (above), about to expunge a terrified mouse labeled "Man's Supremacy," is thundering "Scare ME, will you?"

THE cause of the oppressed Negro was pleaded by William E. B. Du Bois and other founders of the National Association for the Advancement of Colored People. While the fight against the restrictions on immigration aroused some interest, the plight of the Negro scarcely was noticed. Most Americans in the early '20s felt that the progressive years had accomplished all the reforms the country needed—indeed, perhaps more than it needed. To the average man—and the average politician—there were no issues left to fight.

In comparison with what had gone before, and what was to come after, political debate in the '20s was sterile. One of the few questions that aroused tempers was whether or not something should be done for agriculture. Encouraged by wartime demand and high prices, farmers had borrowed heavily to buy land and machinery. When the war ended, the Allies suddenly stopped buying food, the American government ended farm subsidies and the farmers found themselves with huge surpluses. Prices plummeted. Desperate farmers planted still more in an effort to make enough to pay their debts, and the agricultural depression became chronic. Through farm bureaus, which the Agriculture Department had originally set up to teach new techniques, farmers came together, discussed their common plight and agreed that the only remedy lay in legislation.

In the past farmers had sponsored political parties like the Populists to press their demands. This they continued to do in the Farmer-Labor party. But now they took a leaf from the practices of other single-interest groups and set up a lobby, the American Farm Bureau Federation. With agents in Washington and state capitals, the federation in turn forged a farm bloc in Congress. Beginning in 1924 farm representatives worked at every legislative session and every political convention for passage of the McNary-Haugen plan, named for the senator and representative who kept it before Congress.

Though presented in versions differing from year to year, the essence of the plan was that the government buy enough farm produce to level out supply and demand at prices that would give farmers a reasonable income. Members of the farm bloc pleaded with passion, ringing the changes on old slogans about the farmer's importance in society and the moral superiority of the tiller of the soil. But the plain fact was that farmers were finally using the technique that had worked so well in the past to secure special treatment for other pressure groups. To a certain extent they succeeded: They secured tariffs intended to protect American farm products and legislation that eased farm credit. Of greater significance was the effect of their repeated demands for assistance in preparing the way for the agricultural measures of the New Deal.

But the prevailing mood of public apathy was not dispelled by debate over the tariff or taxes or other matters raised by congressmen and presidential candidates. Committed to a tradition of protectionism, Republicans worked to restore the duties that Democrats had reduced. Under the Fordney-McCumber tariff of 1922, American businessmen lobbied for and got schedules designed to keep out most foreign manufactures and raw materials. By hindsight, this policy was probably a contributing factor to the economic collapse that came in 1929. When the increased tariffs were imposed, however, Republicans and many Democrats thought that protective duties were helping to sustain the prosperity that the country appeared to be enjoying. This belief was so pervasive that Congress' response to the Depression was to pass the Hawley-Smoot bill that imposed exorbitant tariff rates.

Primaries, conventions and elections went on from 1920 to 1930, of course, with as much color in the parades, as much frenzy in the rallies and as much steam as ever in the oratory. But what candidates talked about were less political issues than matters of personality. They ran as enemies of corruption and advocates of prosperity; they emphasized their private views on prohibition, religion and morality. La Follette, rallying reform groups, helped establish a Progressive party and ran as its candidate for President in 1924. He won nearly five million votes, but the man who beat him, Calvin Coolidge, had a clear plurality over both La Follette and the Democrat John W. Davis.

The apathy about issues was paralleled by the drabness of the important political personalities. It is a matter of wonder that presidential campaign workers could have battled with such passion for Harding and Coolidge, James M. Cox and John W. Davis. Nor, on the whole, were candidates for state office more inspiring types. There were exceptions: Al Smith, the boy from New York City's Lower East Side who rose to be a Tammany leader and then Democratic Governor of New York, enlivened presidential politics in 1928. Smith's successor, Franklin D. Roosevelt, who had seemed a frivolous young man when he was defeated for Vice President on the Democratic ticket in 1920, became a tough, magnetic leader after his crippling attack of polio.

In Louisiana there was Huey Long, who came out of the canebrakes to become a dictatorial governor in 1928 and to prove that Mussolini's takeover in Italy could be duplicated in America. But there were few such exceptions good or bad; most men in politics belonged to the group that a Republican senator described when he explained how Harding came to be his party's

NOTABLES OF THE '20s
DRAWN WITH SLY WIT

On its 40th birthday, the former "Life" (a magazine of political satire and humor until 1936) caricatured "a few friends and members of the immediate family." The "family" was made up of the leading public figures of 1923. From left are: bushy-browed Senator Borah, child actor Jackie Coogan, Secretary of State Hughes, Vice President Coolidge, Mr. Harding and "The Chief Executive" (a sly poke at the ambitious lady in the White House), Senator Lodge, Elihu Root, Chief Justice William Howard Taft and Senator Oscar W. Underwood of Alabama.

nominee in 1920. "This year we had a lot of second-raters," he said. "Harding is no world-beater. But he's the best of the second-raters."

In that particular case, the senator was wrong. Harding proved in fact one of the worst of second-raters. A small-town newspaper publisher with a handsome profile, a beaming smile and a flair for making friends, he had risen to the Senate by dutifully serving Ohio's Republican machine. Despite his undistinguished record, some cronies started to boom him for the presidency. There were many abler Republicans available, among them General Leonard Wood, Senator Hiram Johnson and Governor Frank Lowden of Illinois. But Harding's friend and manager, Harry M. Daugherty, foresaw that these candidates would become deadlocked. As early as February 1920 he predicted that "about eleven minutes after two, Friday morning of the convention, when ten or twenty weary men are sitting around a table, someone will say, 'Who will we nominate?' At that decisive time the friends of Harding will suggest him and can well afford to abide by the result."

This was almost exactly what happened. On Friday, the third day of the convention, in a suite—later known as the "smoke-filled room"—in Chicago's Blackstone Hotel, there gathered Senators Lodge, Brandegee and Curtis, together with the waspish editor, George Harvey, whose magazine had published some of the most vitriolic criticisms of Wilson's foreign policies, and other G.O.P. stalwarts. These men wanted a man they could control, and they settled on Harding as the most malleable of the candidates. The kingmakers called him in and discreetly inquired whether a campaign might bring to light any scandals in his past. Upon being assured that there were none, they passed the word to the delegates. The next day Harding was nominated.

Harding's oratory, said Democrat William Gibbs McAdoo, gave "the impression of an army of pompous phrases moving over the landscape in search of an idea; sometimes these meandering words would actually capture a straggling thought and bear it triumphantly, a prisoner in their midst, until it died of servitude and overwork." Harding himself said he liked to "bloviate," a slang term meaning to talk grandiloquently.

But his vague and soothing clichés seemed just what the people wanted. For eight years Americans had heard Wilson's sermons on duty, obligation and national mission. They had responded to his New Freedom, his appeals for further domestic reforms, his summons to a world struggle for democracy

Hiram W. Johnson, a maverick Republican who had no qualms about attacking members of his party, called Borah our "spearless leader" and President Taft "the most pitiful figure in American history." Johnson, who flirted with his wife in sign language while he spoke in Congress, had a singularly untaxing hobby: he sat for hours watching his flowers grow.

and his demand for force without stint or limit. The strain had grown nearly unbearable. "Getting and spending" now described their aspirations.

In the aftermath of the armistice, when a number of labor unions went on strike to fight wage cuts or wholesale layoffs, there was widespread fear of a Bolshevik conspiracy like that which had captured Russia. Apprehension increased after unions in Seattle co-operated in a general strike, a phenomenon new to America, and after Boston policemen staged a walkout that left the citizens of that historic city temporarily unprotected. These strikes coincided with a sudden outbreak of anarchist violence. Several bombings occurred, including one at the home of United States Attorney General A. Mitchell Palmer. But for the sloppiness of the senders, whose packages were set aside for insufficient postage, and the vigilance of a post-office clerk who examined the segregated boxes, bombs would have gone through the mails to J. P. Morgan, John D. Rockefeller, Secretary of Labor William B. Wilson, Justice Oliver Wendell Holmes Jr. and others.

Vigilance committees rounded up radicals. Attorney General Palmer raided immigrant neighborhoods and jailed about 4,000 aliens, some of whom he had deported on trumped-up charges. All of this went on for six months, from November 1919 until the spring of 1920. Then, suddenly, people seemed to realize how foolishly they had been behaving ever since the war had begun. Hysteria at last subsided. The country appeared all at once to have grown tired of being stirred up by political leaders. Harding, promising a return to "normalcy" (a word he coined), seemed just the man to supply it.

HE had no desire to be a strong President. He was devoid of ideas. He told one of his secretaries: "I can't make a damn thing out of this tax problem. . . . I listen to one side and they seem right, and then—God—I talk to the other side and they seem just as right, and here I am where I started. I know somewhere there is a book that will give me the truth, but hell! I couldn't read the book." Harding had no program, no plan, no mission. His only discernible aim as President was to be loved.

He promised to form an Administration of the "most experienced minds" in the country. In naming Hughes Secretary of State, Henry Wallace Secretary of Agriculture (his son would hold the same position under the New Deal) and Herbert Hoover Secretary of Commerce, he seemed to be carrying out this pledge. It was partly blind luck that he did so; Harding's first choice for Secretary of State had been Senator Albert Fall, a bluff rancher from New Mexico. However, political expediency dictated the appointment of Hughes, from populous New York. Fall became Secretary of the Interior. Harding had also considered George Harvey for the post. But Harvey chose instead to go to London as ambassador. Andrew Mellon was another good appointment, or so it seemed at the time. Mellon, who retained his post under both Coolidge and Hoover, was long described as the greatest Secretary of the Treasury since Alexander Hamilton—until the Depression revealed that Gulf Oil, Alcoa and other Mellon interests had been among the objects of his beneficences.

A number of Harding's appointments aroused misgivings even at the outset. Harding's campaign manager, Harry Daugherty, was named Attorney General. Daugherty was primarily a political fixer with skimpy legal experience. He had won his most celebrated case, the pardon appeal of a stock swindler, Charles W. Morse, by pleading that Morse was dying of an incurable

Will Rogers said, "I never met a man I didn't like," but issues enraged him. Two boxers earned $309,000 when Pershing was to be retired at half salary. "Fight for yourself instead of for your country," Rogers cried. "My Lord, can't our Government do something for a man who is not a Politician?"

disease. As it turned out, Morse had eaten a bar of soap and hoaxed or bribed government physicians to secure the dire diagnosis. Morse lived on for 15 years, plying his old trade.

From the beginning, reporters in Washington were aware of a certain moral laxity pervading the Harding Administration. Two or three times a week a group gathered at the White House for high-stakes poker games. Though decorum was preserved in the public rooms on the first floor, things upstairs were different. Visiting her childhood home, Alice Roosevelt Longworth saw "the study . . . filled with cronies . . . the air heavy with tobacco smoke, trays with bottles containing every imaginable brand of whiskey stood about, cards and poker chips ready at hand—a general atmosphere of waistcoat unbuttoned, feet on the desk, and the spittoon alongside."

Elsewhere, there was revelry on various levels. Ned McLean, the heir to a newspaper empire and one of those friends with whom, it was said, the President found "complete mental relaxation," gave lavish, long-night parties at which, following the White House model, the prohibition amendment was ignored. At a dwelling on K Street, celebrated later as the "little green house," there was continuous celebration: Card games were always in progress, the bar never closed, girls came in and out on call, and underworld figures met with politicians to discuss such matters as pardons, paroles and withdrawal certificates permitting the purchase of alcohol for industrial or pharmaceutical use. The host here was Howard Mannington, who held no office but who was an old friend of Harding's and an inner member of what was called the "Ohio Gang." Surgeon-General Sawyer and many others who sat in on White House poker games were frequent visitors at K Street. The Attorney General came seldom if at all, but his close friend Jesse Smith was a regular and was often heard humming in his husky voice, "Good God! How the money rolls in!"

The press knew about these high jinks but at first kept quiet. Congressmen unfriendly to the Administration were not so tactful and asked pointed questions about pardons. Harding, a man with no malice in his soul, had released from prison many German-Americans, pacifists and radicals (including Socialist Eugene V. Debs) jailed under wartime laws. These compassionate acts earned more praise than criticism; but nasty rumors arose when the penitentiary doors opened for tax evaders and liquor law violators, including George Remus, the nationally known "King of the Bootleggers." The administration of federal prisons came under scrutiny when an investigation of large-scale narcotics traffic among inmates of the penitentiary at Atlanta was blocked by the superintendent of federal prisons, Harding's brother-in-law.

I N 1922, after the Administration had been in office a little over a year and a half, a scandal finally broke into the open. One of Harding's closest friends, Charles R. Forbes, a man with an extremely spotty past, was director of the Veterans' Bureau. Harding approved without question whatever Forbes proposed, and Forbes promptly cashed in on his opportunities. He made a deal with a St. Louis building firm giving him a substantial commission on new hospitals. To a Boston concern he sold some three million dollars' worth of bed sheets, gauze and other supplies for about $600,000.

Only when the evidence against Forbes became overwhelming was Harding convinced that Forbes had to go. According to a man who was a witness to the President's last meeting with Forbes, Harding held his former friend by

Andrew Mellon was self-conscious about the immensity of his fortune. Although he ultimately acquired paintings worth more than $50 million, he once declined to buy a picture because an acquaintance remarked: "I used to think it'd be swell to have persons hear I'd paid $100,000 for a picture."

After Harding died, Nan Britton, who claimed he fathered her illegitimate child, wrote the book that caused the scandal of the decade: "The President's Daughter." Her purpose, besides getting a tenth of Harding's estate, was to gain "social recognization . . . of all children . . . born of wedlock [sic]."

the neck and shouted at him, "You yellow rat! You double-crossing bastard!" Then the entire mess came into the open. Charles F. Cramer, the counsel for the Veterans' Bureau, was deeply involved, and in March 1923 he shot himself.

Cramer's was not the only death. Concerned over rumors of Jesse Smith's activities in the "little green house," Harding suggested to Daugherty that he end the friendship. The Attorney General told Jesse to go home. Big, awkward, flabby, with a vacant face, eyes out of plumb and spluttering speech, Jesse had been a dry goods merchant back in Washington Court House, Ohio. In the national capital he was a chum of the great, and the money was good. He loved it. Though he obeyed his friend's order, he found that he could not stand exile. He bought a gun, returned to Washington, went to Daugherty's apartment and killed himself. Because Smith was so well known, the sensation was even greater than that caused by Cramer's suicide. Before his death Jesse had paused to burn a quantity of his own and the Attorney General's private papers. Washington gossip whispered murder.

Forbes's fall, the two suicides and rumors about Daugherty were terrible blows to Harding. He still went to the golf course several times a week, but he no longer played all 18 holes. He talked of giving up liquor. Some of those who saw him in June 1923, just before he left on a cross-country tour, thought his health might be failing.

The trip was supposed to invigorate him. He was in his element, "bloviating" to friendly crowds at whistle-stop towns. But the President remained overwrought, unable to relax. A sea voyage to Alaska and back failed to help. After a day of ceremonies in Seattle, he suffered what was first diagnosed as acute indigestion but was probably a coronary seizure. In San Francisco he came down with pneumonia. For nearly a week he lay in bed. Although his lungs began to clear, a blood clot formed in his brain. On August 2 he died.

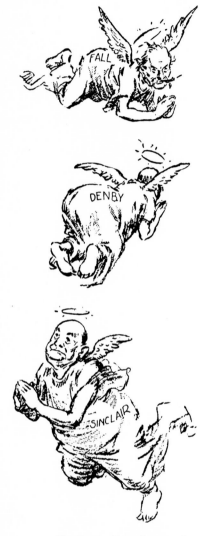

The Teapot Dome hearings became pitifully ludicrous as the principals tried to cover their sullied past. The "whiter than snow" cherubs above are Interior Secretary Fall, Navy Secretary Denby and oilman Sinclair. Once the defense actually claimed that a witness who thought he heard of a $68,000 bribe had really heard the phrase "six to eight cows."

THERE was mourning all across the country, for Harding, like McKinley, had been much loved and little hated. But the mourning was short-lived. In Washington Senator Thomas J. Walsh of Montana was digging into scandals much more serious than those in the Veterans' Bureau. Bit by bit, Walsh's investigations uncovered evidence that indicated wrongdoings by Interior Secretary Fall. Fall had talked Harding into transferring to his department control over oil-rich lands that Congress had set aside as naval reserves. The Secretary also abused his authority to permit private oil companies to drill on the reserves by granting secret leases without competitive bidding. Fall had used this power to lease the Elk Hills reserve in California to Edward L. Doheny of the Pan-American Petroleum Company and the Teapot Dome reserve in Wyoming to Harry F. Sinclair of Mammoth Oil. Coincidentally, the Secretary himself had managed somehow to pay off old debts and bank large sums of money. Walsh, tireless, patient and thorough, probed this coincidence.

At first Fall claimed to have had a $100,000 loan from Ned McLean, a story that McLean confirmed. But, when inconsistencies developed, McLean backtracked. He had lent Fall such a sum, he said, but had been repaid almost immediately; it turned out that McLean had never cashed Fall's checks. Then Doheny finally admitted that he had loaned the money, but he insisted that it was an ordinary business loan that had no connection with oil. Well, perhaps it wasn't an entirely orthodox loan; Doheny, who called himself an "old-time, impulsive, irresponsible, improvident sort of a prospector," confessed that he and Fall had not observed all the customary formalities. Fall had simply given Doheny an IOU which Doheny had then torn in half so that it would remain a gentleman's agreement and not a legally enforceable note. The money itself had not been paid to Fall by check; Doheny's son had carried it, in cash, in a small black satchel.

What little credence this tale might have inspired was dissipated when Walsh discovered that Fall had also come into possession of $233,000 worth of numbered Liberty Bonds. When their history was traced, they proved to have belonged to a Canadian corporation, the Continental Trading Company, owned in large part by Harry Sinclair. This was enough. Fall was tried and eventually went to prison for taking bribes. The oil leases were voided.

Forbes was sent to the penitentiary for his thievery. Then it was Daugherty's turn. Walsh's fellow senator from Montana, Burton K. Wheeler, discovered that Daugherty had banked $75,000 in one of his accounts while earning a salary of $12,000 a year and living sumptuously. At his trial Daugherty refused to testify, hinting that he was trying to protect the reputation of the dead President. Two successive juries disagreed, and Daugherty escaped jail.

Daugherty's insinuations turned suspicion toward Harding, especially when it was discovered that the President had been a heavy speculator in the stock market. As the revelations tumbled in, the country learned that Harding had kept a mistress, held trysts with her in the White House and probably fathered her illegitimate child. F.B.I. agent Gaston B. Means suggested that Harding had not died naturally but had been poisoned by his jealous wife. Although Means was a proven swindler, his tales won wide belief. There has never been proof that Harding took a penny in graft; the worst that can be said with certainty is that he was merely a weak man with poor judgment. Nevertheless the public found it possible to believe almost anything of him and his Administration.

The man who succeeded him could not have presented a sharper contrast. Coolidge had his faults. He lost his temper easily and he was given to playing cruel practical jokes on his family, servants and Secret Service guards. But outwardly he seemed an embodiment of the Puritan virtues. No one who looked at Coolidge's pinched face or heard his dry Yankee voice could imagine him straying from the straight and narrow or countenancing immorality in anyone else. He gradually cleaned out Harding's worst appointees and replaced them with men of unquestionable integrity. For example, Harlan F. Stone, who would later be a distinguished Chief Justice of the Supreme Court, became Attorney General. The weakness of Coolidge's Administration was to be not in its moral fiber but in its vision. The President himself was to say that "this is a business country; it wants a business government," and that "the man who builds a factory builds a temple. . . . The man who works there worships there."

UNLIKE Roosevelt and Wilson, who dominated their eras, neither Harding nor Coolidge cut much of a figure in his country's life. The minds of Americans were not on legislative matters or contests for office. People were preoccupied with ways of making money, with prohibition, sports and amusements and, sometimes, with questions of race or religion. Perhaps in that smug, self-centered time, there was little that any man could have done to shake the prosperous country out of its complacency.

Attorney General Daugherty, a notorious influence peddler in Harding's ill-starred Administration, is shown here trying to conceal his record from Uncle Sam. When he came under attack in 1922, Daugherty said (with unintentional irony), "I wouldn't have given thirty cents for the office of Attorney General, but I wouldn't surrender it for a million dollars."

Boom years for the gas buggies

I THINK people are going to buy quite a passel of these gasoline buggies."
So said Frank Phillips in 1904; and, backing his hunch, he later founded
the Phillips Petroleum Company to market the gas "to make 'em go." But
even pioneers like Phillips were astounded by the fantastic growth of motoring after World War I. Between 1920 and 1929 the number of registered cars
jumped from eight million to 23 million. In 1904 only 12,000 workers had
been directly employed in the auto industry; 25 years later 471,000 were
producing cars, and countless thousands more were supplying auto services.

As this revolution on wheels swept over America, a new way of life came
with it. City and country were drawn together by a spreading network of
hard-surfaced roads; new factories and pleasant suburbs flourished where
a few years before there had been inaccessible wilderness. Growth fed on
growth: more cars brought more roads, more jobs, higher wages—and a greater demand for cars. Within one generation, traffic jams replaced mudholes
as the bane of American motorists. Humorist Will Rogers, saluting the genius whose "flivver" (overleaf) had started all this, declared whimsically: "So
good luck, Mr. Ford. It will take a hundred years to tell whether you have
helped us or hurt us, but you certainly didn't leave us like you found us."

STUCK IN THE MUD, intrepid travelers (left) leave their car
on a Nebraska road in 1915. In that year of primitive motoring, unpaved roads were a common hazard even in urban areas.

IN GLEAMING ARRAY, early auto accessories (opposite)—lights,
hubcaps, license plates, a bulb horn—suggest the rapid improvements that led up to the motoring boom of the 1920s.

AT REST, the Model T is awkward and seven feet high. But most buyers agreed with the Ford dealer who called it "the greatest creation in automobiles ever placed before a people."

The Model T: noisy, bouncy, balky and indestructible

AT PLAY, a Tin Lizzie climbs a flight of stairs on a 41 per cent grade. The car's high clearance and rugged construction were carefully engineered for the rutted dirt roads it had to use.

AT WORK, a Ford serves as a jitney bus, carrying passengers over a regular route for a nickel, or "jitney." Certain transit companies went to court to squelch such "unfair competition."

Henry Ford's Model T could develop only 20 horsepower and a bone-rattling top speed of 45 miles per hour. It was tricky to operate, possessing three pedals (clutch, reverse and brake), a lever with three positions (high gear, neutral and brake) and a radiator that often boiled over. But, true to the first Ford advertisement, it was "designed for everyday wear and tear," and its construction was so simple that many minor repairs could be made with hairpins, baling wire and chewing gum.

This indestructible contraption, affectionately called the "Tin Lizzie," was built between 1908 and 1927. As its numbers increased (to 15 million), its price decreased (from $850 for a touring car in 1908 to $290 in 1924). It was the first reliable car within easy reach of most wage earners. One of the numerous jokes told by proud owners went: "The Model T is a good car—a rattling good car."

REPLACING THE HORSE, Model Ts crowd the main street of Henderson, Texas, in the mid-1920s. Farmers and ranchers, who had avoided long trips away from home by horse-drawn wagon, now began making regular visits to such rural towns for socializing as well as business. Back at the ranch, they harnessed the car's power to grind feed, pump water and cut wood.

Artist James Montgomery Flagg and Cadillac

Actor Gary Cooper at the wheel of his high-powered, precision-built 1931 Duesenberg

An elegant Chrysler Custom Imperial Landau, specially built in 1932 for the company's founder and president, Walter P. Chrysler

Gangster Al Capone's bulletproof Cadillac, on display as a curiosity

Dancer Gilda Gray and her expensive Hispano-Suiza limousine

Actress Gloria Swanson in her Italian-built Lancia

Singer Al Jolson with his wife, actress Ruby Keeler, in their Mercedes-Benz

An automobile for every taste and pocketbook

Governor Al Smith goes politicking in a 1928 Packard

WHILE standardized economy cars were produced by the millions, more elaborate makes and models were available to prospective buyers who could afford to be different. Cadillac, Packard, Stutz and Lincoln offered fine autos—low-slung sports models, high-speed touring cars, ponderous limousines. For those who desired even grander cars, Bugatti, Duesenberg and Hispano-Suiza would assemble unique models according to the customer's choice of motor, chassis and body work; and they would paint the final product in such exotic colors as "Florentine cream" and "Versailles violet." The rich and the famous proudly indulged their tastes: An Asian prince owned as many as 50 Rolls-Royces, and Walter P. Chrysler's personal car *(opposite, center)* was not the only one with a bar for serving drinks in transit.

President Warren Harding in a Packard after his 1921 inauguration

Football coach Knute Rockne and his namesake, the Rockne Six

75

IMPROVED GASOLINE attracts motorists to a Dayton, Ohio, station, which in 1923 became the first to offer ethyl. This new gas gave more power and was premium-priced at 25 cents a gallon. Before 1913, when gas stations began spreading, car owners bought fuel from stores or local oil companies, which provided regular customers with a tank for back-yard storage.

A section of the Lincoln Highway is marked by workmen operating from Autocar trucks. The group which proposed this transcontinental

A nation spreading out along new highways

Highway building boomed with the tremendous increase in cars. In 1909 the United States had only 725 miles of paved rural roads, but by 1930 more than 100,000 miles of such roads crisscrossed the nation. Deserts and mountains became shortcuts; great tunnels, bridges and multilane highways were being built to relieve the mounting pressure of auto traffic in urban areas.

Where the road builders passed, new businesses grew up in profusion. The first modern filling stations were opened by 1913; by 1929 there were 121,500 of them. Trucking services proliferated. In 1904 only 700 trucks were registered in the United States; by 1929 there were 3.4 million. Cities and towns were served by taxis *(right)*, connected by bus lines, dotted with parking lots, garages and automatic traffic lights. By 1930 most major highways bore unmistakable evidence of modern times: billboards, hotdog stands, diners, tourist cabins.

SQUARE AND STURDY, this 1922 Checker Cab is one of the earliest of special-bodied taxis. The first cabs were simply standard touring cars which liverymen used to haul fares.

highway publicized the need for better roads and encouraged local co-operation. Congress passed the first Federal Aid Road Act in 1916.

A SEDAN FOR THE FAMILY, this 1929 Chevrolet stands ready for the road. The model, known as the "cast iron wonder," supplanted the Ford as the most popular of low-priced cars.

Rediscovering America
in the family car

IN the decade that followed the First World War, the automobile became a national institution. Americans spent an estimated $30 billion on cars. Mass production, installment-plan buying and the development of the second-hand car market put serviceable transportation within reach of most families. The auto freed millions of Americans from the front porch on Sundays; and, to the alarm of many, it shifted the scene of courtship from the parlor to the country lane.

Overjoyed by their new mobility, car owners took to the road in a mass rediscovery of America. In 1924 motorists traveled more than 100 billion miles on the nation's highways. People of all classes and from all parts of the country mingled in roadside restaurants, hotels and tourist camps. They honked at each other in traffic jams, helped each other change flat tires, grew familiar with many regional accents and customs.

By 1930 sociologists and psychologists had advanced many explanations for the phenomenal success of the automobile. Almost every motorist had his own opinion. In a widely reported interview, a farmer's wife was asked why her family owned a car but not a bathtub. She replied briskly, "You can't go to town in a bathtub."

PORTENDING TROUBLE, an early traffic jam halts motorists in the '20s. Despite vast road projects, building lagged behind car sales, making for bigger traffic jams.

4. THE BUSINESS OF AMERICA

AMERICA in the '20s is remembered as a land of prosperity. A summary review of the statistics of the time confirms this impression. Although the beginning of the decade saw a sharp recession, conditions quickly picked up, and almost every sector of the economy except agriculture improved. Industrial production climbed nearly 50 per cent between 1920 and 1929; the national income grew from $79.1 billion to almost $88 billion. Since price levels actually declined a bit, those extra dollars bought more. And on every hand were more things to buy—automobiles, bungalows in mushrooming real-estate developments, home appliances, out-of-season foods kept fresh by refrigeration. Prosperity, to be sure, was spread unevenly, but for people with money in the bank, America in the '20s was a wonderland.

The marvelous aspects of the '20s stemmed, in large part, from the spectacular growth of new industries. Americans of that time nodded approval to President Coolidge's remark that "the chief business of the American people is business." The heroes of the '20s were not politicians, thinkers or artists, but businessmen like Henry Ford and Samuel Insull, corporations like General Motors and Metro-Goldwyn-Mayer.

Although Ford was pre-eminently the symbol of the automobile industry, at the turn of the century he had been only one of a number of mechanics, engineers and manufacturers excited by the challenge of the horseless carriage. George N. Pierce of Buffalo moved from bird cages and refrigerators

A PRO-BUSINESS PRESIDENT, Calvin Coolidge is seen after he left the White House. By not seeking a second full term he escaped the "bust" that stigmatized his successor.

After producing Model Ts for 19 years, Henry Ford gave the public a new design. In 1927 a cartoonist pictured him as a mother hen hatching the new Model A at his Dearborn plant. Though the production change-over cost about $250 million, he said, "We paid no attention to the cost. . . . When you are thinking about things like that you can't do a good job."

to bicycles to the Pierce-Arrow. The Studebaker brothers of South Bend had a world reputation for fine wagons and carriages that helped the sale of their first autos. Walter Chrysler, a railroad superintendent, became fascinated at an automobile exhibit, withdrew his life savings of $700, borrowed another $4,300 and bought a car. When he got it home, he took it apart and found out how it worked. A few years later he went to work for the Buick Motor Company, even though it meant a 50 per cent cut in pay.

MANY of these pioneers had a brief period of glory and then disappeared into the footnotes of automotive histories. Ford, however, remained a major figure in the industry practically from the beginning. Born in 1863 on a Michigan farm, he had tinkered with machines from childhood. He moved to Detroit in 1879, qualified as a machinist and later became chief engineer of an electric-light company. Before the 20th Century opened, his hobby of building cars had turned into a full-time occupation.

In 1902 he pitted his "999," described as "a low, rakish looking craft [that] makes more noise than a freight train," against Alexander Winton's record-setting racer. Reluctant to race, Ford had hired a cigar-chewing daredevil named Barney Oldfield. "He had never driven a motor car," Ford said later, "but he . . . said he would try anything once." After a few weeks of practice, Oldfield roared around the course at almost 55 miles an hour, won the race and began the career as a racing driver that for decades made his name synonymous with speed. The prestige that Ford gained was even greater.

Ford, always somewhat of a zealot, had visions far loftier than winning races. His ambition was to make the largest number of cars at the lowest possible price. Disregarding the forecasts that the future belonged to the makers of heavy luxury cars, Ford persisted in his dream. In 1908 he first produced the Model T, the "Tin Lizzie," a car that was light, durable, simple and relatively cheap. Within a few years he had adopted mass-production and assembly-line techniques that helped reduce the price.

In an affectionate recollection of the miraculous aspects of the Model T, Lee Strout White has written in his book *Farewell to Model T:*

> To get under way you simply hooked the third finger of the right hand around a lever on the steering column, pulled down hard, and shoved your foot forcibly against the low-speed pedal. These were simple, positive motions; the car responded by lunging forward with a roar. After a few seconds of this turmoil, you took your foot off the pedal, eased up a mite on the throttle, and the car, possessed of two forward speeds, catapulted directly into high with a series of ugly jerks and was off on its glorious errand. The abruptness of this departure was never equalled in other cars of this period. . . .

The public response to this revolutionary vehicle was immediate. More than 10,000 Model Ts were sold in the first year; more than 150,000 in 1912-1913; almost one million in 1920-1921. By 1914 nearly half the cars sold annually in the United States were Fords.

Henry Ford became a folk hero. Not only had he defied the pundits of his industry to make a product for the common people, but he had gone to war against a combine that claimed an automotive patent monopoly, fought and won his case in the courts, and thus singlehandedly had slain a would-be trust. In 1914 Ford suddenly announced that the basic wage in his plant would be five dollars a day. This pay, far above the national average, may have been meant to forestall union organizers, cut down absenteeism, share company profits or even contribute toward the creation of new markets for Model Ts. But Henry Ford seldom explained why he did anything, and no one was ever much good at divining his motives. Whatever was in his mind, the public thought of him as a mechanical genius, a production wizard, a foe of the trusts, a champion of the little man and a friend of labor.

Afterward the glitter of his fame was somewhat tarnished. While he had remarkable talents, his powers were intuitive rather than rational, and when he strayed from automobile-making, he was apt to stumble. Abhorring war, he spent $400,000 on a "peace ship," loaded it with pacifists and sailed for Europe in 1915 in an effort to bring the belligerents to terms. The attempt failed and brought on Ford a certain amount of ridicule.

In 1918 he ran for the Senate, and during his campaign his opponents recalled his 1916 statement that he had seldom voted (and then only "because Mrs. Ford drove me to do it"). Ford lost to Republican Truman H. Newberry and emerged angry. Private detectives gathered for him evidence that Newberry had violated the Federal Corrupt Practices Act. Although Newberry was found guilty, the verdict was reversed on appeal.

In 1916 Ford sued the Chicago *Tribune* for calling him an anarchist. When the case was tried in 1919, Ford demonstrated his ignorance. On the stand, among other egregious errors, he named 1812 as the year of the American Revolution and identified Benedict Arnold as a writer. These lapses should not have been surprising; in 1916 he had said: "History is more or less bunk." In 1918 he bought a newspaper, the Dearborn *Independent*, in which his opinions were reflected. These were often foolish and sometimes vicious, especially when he became convinced of the existence of a "Jewish conspiracy" and repeated long discredited anti-Semitic slanders.

S USPICIOUS and self-willed, Ford bought out his original partners, turning his half-billion-dollar company into a family property. Able but independent men like William S. Knudsen left to work for other manufacturers. Despite clear evidence that enterprising competitors were taking away customers, Ford would not hear of major changes in the Model T; not until 1925 would he offer a choice of colors. Customers could have their Model Ts in any shade, he snorted, "so long as it is black." By 1926 Chevrolet was fast overtaking Ford in sales. He finally brought out the Model A in 1928, but he could recapture only part of the market he had lost to Chevrolet.

None of these setbacks had as much effect on Ford's standing with the public as might have been expected. Ford engaged William J. Cameron, a newspaperman, who made it his business to convince the public that Ford was an inspired tinkerer, the living proof of the old saw about the better mousetrap, the symbol of an industry that was transforming the country, a man whose inner grace was manifest in the fact that his family's income was nine million dollars a year.

Many other important figures in the automobile industry were, like Ford, more at home with tools than ledgers. But there was one man, in no way typical of the run of automobile tycoons, who deserved more fame than he achieved. William Crapo Durant, who created General Motors, was strictly a promoter. A well-to-do carriage maker in Flint, Michigan, Durant took over

Behind these car emblems were complex shifts of ownership that typified the expanding auto industry. Buick, taken over by W. C. Durant, became the cornerstone of General Motors. W. P. Chrysler designed a new model for Maxwell, started Chrysler and acquired Dodge. The Pierce-Arrow Company passed from hand to hand until it went out of business in 1938.

"Speed demon" Barney Oldfield set a stunning record of 64.5 mph in 1903 driving the Ford 999. His familiar cigar served a practical purpose: By biting down on it during his jarring rides, he managed to keep his teeth intact. After leaving racing he turned businessman, promoting, among other things, a code of ethics for the Barney Oldfield Registered Hitch-hikers, Inc.

the young, undercapitalized Buick company in 1904. On this foundation, and at a time when the automobile was still a novelty, Durant constructed the concept of a great combination of auto companies. By 1910 he had brought together 12 auto producers, including Oldsmobile, Oakland (later Pontiac) and Cadillac, as the General Motors Company. When he tried to buy out Ford, the story goes that Ford was willing, but demanded payment of eight million dollars in cash. Durant had no such liquid reserve, and the deal fell through.

Rapid expansion left the company badly undercapitalized, and by 1910 General Motors was taken over by bankers. Henry M. Leland, founder of Cadillac, and his son Wilfred talked the bankers out of dissolving the company; the price was the ousting of Durant. His successor, Boston financier James J. Storrow, worked closely with Charles W. Nash, a superb organizer. They sold off unprofitable firms until only Cadillac, Buick, Oldsmobile, Oakland, the General Motors Truck Company and a few subsidiaries remained.

Meanwhile Durant had formed a new company to produce a low-cost car designed by Louis Chevrolet, a Swiss-born mechanic and auto racer. Using all his promoting skills, Durant pyramided the capital of the new venture to $80 million. Then, with Chevrolet shares as his currency, he quietly bought up General Motors stock. By 1916 he was able to regain control.

For five hectic years Durant returned to the pursuit of his dream. He bought up one company after another, among them the Fisher Body Company, the Remy Electric Company and the Dayton Engineering Laboratories Company (DELCO), whose brilliant head, Charles F. "Boss" Kettering, had developed the self-starter. Durant added parts firms, foreign subsidiaries and the General Motors Acceptance Corporation, a company that financed the time-payment purchases of his autos. He also went into side lines such as the Frigidaire Corporation. By 1920 General Motors was an empire. Its divisions turned out models in a dozen different price ranges; it owned many of its suppliers; its network of dealerships portended a serious threat to Ford.

During the recession of 1920, however, the shaky nature of many of Durant's personal investments again put General Motors in jeopardy. This time it was rescued by the vast resources of the Du Pont family. But Durant had to go.

He made one more effort to build an empire. Durant Motors, like GM, offered models running from the low-cost Star through the Durant-Four and the Flint to the luxury-class Locomobile. Despite his efforts, Durant was never able to catch up with GM, Ford and Chrysler, by 1928 the big three of the industry. The stock market crash of 1929 finished him off. Durant disappeared from public view, a bankrupt. Shortly thereafter a reporter who saw him in Asbury Park, New Jersey, published a story that the founder of General Motors had been reduced to sweeping floors for a living. Actually, pioneering at 75 with a suburban supermarket, he was cleaning up for opening day.

DURANT and Ford, so different in outlook, had one quality in common: Each had the distant look of the dreamer. Ford saw the automobile as a vehicle for the masses; he envisioned cars rolling off assembly lines by the hundreds of thousands until, as he predicted to his wife, the streets would be four-deep in traffic. Durant saw something similar. But because he understood the American people far better than did Ford, Durant saw that auto manufacturers would have to turn out a variety of models, make frequent changes and make most sales on credit. To accomplish these things, the industry would have to organize itself not in giant companies but in giant combinations that could take advantage of mass buying, mass production and mass selling while preserving the identities of individual manufacturers.

Between them, Ford and Durant were chiefly responsible for the fact that by 1930 there were over 23 million automobiles in the United States, roughly one car for every five Americans, and that automobile manufacture had become one of the most important basic industries in America.

Much of the business boom was tied to the auto. Steel production more than doubled in the 20 years after the introduction of the Model T; rubber became a billion-dollar industry; refinery output increased more than nine times. The automobile was largely responsible for this growth, as it was, in part, for the spurt of suburban residential and highway construction.

ANOTHER industry that participated in the boom was electric power. From small beginnings in the late 19th Century, the use of this new source of energy pyramided. About six billion kilowatt-hours were consumed in 1902; over 57 billion by 1920; about 118 billion by 1929. One third of all homes had electricity in 1920; two thirds by 1929. Even more spectacular than its rate of growth was the financing of the industry, for between 1922 and 1927 its capitalization increased from $5.3 billion to more than $12 billion.

As Ford and Durant symbolized car making, so did Samuel Insull's name come to be identified with public utilities. After an early and successful career in the East with Thomas Edison, Insull moved to Chicago in 1892, and for most of the next 40 years he and the city were to be indissolubly linked. Exploiting every technological improvement and developing some on his own, he extended central-station electric service through the city and its suburbs, then out to surrounding states and rural areas. He was the first to use giant steam turbine generators, the first to recognize that it would be most efficient if a single system generated all the electricity for home, transportation and industrial use. Insull installed meters and scaled charges so that they bore some relationship to what it cost the company to supply the service. When advances were made, Insull was nearly always in the lead.

As a lean, fast-talking, energetic youth, he seemed the embodiment of drive and ambition. In later years, carrying more pounds, a Teddy Roosevelt mustache hiding the hard lines of his mouth, a beautiful actress for a wife and a publicized role in society, he gave an impression of force.

In financing Insull developed the open-end mortgage. In contrast to traditional mortgages with their fixed total loans and predetermined durations, the open-end mortgage had no limits except the borrower's willingness to borrow and the lender's to lend. Insull pioneered the mass marketing of stocks by offering shares in his utility companies to his customers. Long before most of his counterparts, he accepted the view that certain businesses, especially public utilities, were affected with a public interest. Though interested in profits and seeing to it that his companies did well, he advocated state regulation of utilities as early as 1898.

Insull's company was one of the first to establish a public-relations department, with the job of explaining to the public how utilities operated and how rates were set. He pounded home the message that the more electricity generated, the less the charges needed to be for each kilowatt-hour of output. As he expanded service he lowered rates—a practice that had a good deal to

The well-known trademark of the Fisk Tire Company, seen in this 1921 advertisement, was conceived late one night in 1906. The artist, Burr Giffen, was awakened by a sudden inspiration. He jumped out of bed and quickly sketched the yawning boy in the Dr. Denton sleeping suit. So that no one would miss the point, Fisk added the punning slogan, "Time to re-tire?"

do with both the popularity and the political invulnerability he enjoyed.

By 1929 Insull's fame was as great as that of any man in America. The utilities he controlled included Commonwealth Edison; Public Service of Northern Illinois; Midland Utilities, serving Indiana; and Middle West Utilities, a billion-dollar corporation operating in 32 states. Several of the most powerful banks and brokerage houses of the Midwest were regarded as his instruments. He was at the head of many of Chicago's charitable and civic endeavors, notably the opera. In newspapers and magazines the country over, his words were quoted with approval and awe.

He seemed to have the Midas touch, and financiers who had earlier been hesitant to risk money in electric power now became eager to do so if Insull was involved. Phil McEnroe, his bookkeeper, said, "The bankers would call us up the way the grocer used to call my mamma, and try to push their money at us. . . . 'We have some nice fresh green money today, Mr. Insull. Isn't there something you could use maybe ten million dollars for?'"

In recent years it has been suggested that since Insull had spent so much of his earlier life scrabbling for funds with which to expand, he could not now resist the proffered money. Then, the theory goes, he began to worry that someone might steal his companies from him through surreptitious purchase of these securities. His fear was confirmed when Cyrus Eaton, the Cleveland financier, acquired big blocks of stock in several Insull companies. To protect himself, Insull made use of the financing he had been offered to create investment trusts to buy shares in his own companies. Insull, formerly a manager with some holdings, now became an owner with voting control. Soon there was a pyramid of paper corporations so entangled with one another that it would require weeks of testimony just to suggest the structure.

Financier Samuel Insull, accused of fraud and embezzlement on a grand scale, was eventually acquitted of all the charges, but it took a long struggle. In the mid-'30s he was caricatured (above) as the "Daring Old Man" on the flying trapeze, leaping grimly from trial to trial. "My greatest ambition in life," he said, "is to hand down my name as clean as I received it."

THE stock market crash of 1929 threatened the whole matchstick house. However none of Insull's operating units, as distinguished from his paper superstructure, ever went into bankruptcy. But Insull had powerful enemies who included the old families of Chicago, the reform group in that city and, most important of all, the New York financial community. It was Eaton's pressure, however, that started Insull's downfall. To prevent Eaton from dumping his Insull stock on the depressed market, Insull was forced to buy these shares. For the first time since starting his own business, Insull in 1930 had to go to New York for money. As the market continued to fall, the collateral Insull had put up became insufficient to cover the loans. Consequently the banks took possession of the stock collateral, thereby gaining control of Insull's companies. Then the House of Morgan demanded his resignation. According to one biographer, the new owners pilloried Insull as a scoundrel in order to protect themselves from the anger of badly hurt stockholders.

Franklin D. Roosevelt, campaigning for the presidency in 1932, spoke of "the lone wolf, the unethical competitor, the Ishmael or Insull whose hand is against every man's." In Cook County, Illinois, a Republican state's attorney, desperately seeking to stem a Democratic tide, asked a grand jury to indict Insull for having, by financial manipulation, committed larceny against his own companies. The federal government also indicted him. Insull, vacationing in Paris, fled to Greece, with which the United States had no extradition treaty. Then, forced to move on through American pressure, he was seized in Istanbul and brought home to stand trial.

During the lengthy court proceedings, out of which he emerged acquitted, it became increasingly clear that while Insull had taken advantage of the defects of the system, the system had certainly been faulty; some remedies were supplied by the New Deal legislation of 1934 and later. But there was irony in the fact that though Insull was one of the few businessmen of the '20s who had advocated public accountability of corporations and financiers, his was the name that has remained a synonym for the evils of the old system.

THE motion-picture business was still another of the great industries of the '20s. In the late 1880s Edison, after pioneering electricity, developed a gadget he called the kinetoscope. Projecting a sequence of photographs at such speed that figures seemed to move, it was a great improvement over various earlier attempts of other inventors. The kinetoscope was first put to commercial use in coin-in-the-slot machines. Then "nickelodeons" by the thousands were opened between 1905 and 1910 solely to exhibit the early movies. Meanwhile entrepreneurs, actors, writers and photographers drifted into the business of making films. From simple scenes showing movement such as that of an onrushing locomotive, the movie makers advanced to photoplays lasting nearly a quarter of an hour. These short narratives in time were supplanted by the features that ran for an hour or more.

It was extraordinary how rapidly the business developed. Even before 1918 the audience for movies totaled tens of millions. Film companies proliferated. When the Motion Picture Patents Company attempted to monopolize the industry, claiming that it had the exclusive right to the patents taken out by Edison and others, many independent producers shifted their operations to Southern California. There they enjoyed the double advantage of dependably sunny weather and, when process servers and detectives appeared, the proximity of asylum across the nearby Mexican border. Ultimately the trust failed in its efforts. In the meantime certain of the independents, like Adolph Zukor's Paramount Pictures Corporation, Carl Laemmle's Universal Film Company, and the Fox and Mutual companies, grew to substantial size; some of them went beyond producing pictures to owning chains of theaters in which their products were shown.

Until 1910 performers could be identified only as the "Biograph Girl" or the "Man with the Sad Eyes," etc. But when Carl Laemmle bought the contract of the "Biograph Girl," Florence Lawrence, he decided to advertise her by name, and arranged for her to make a personal appearance in St. Louis. Adoring fans tore the buttons from her coat, box-office receipts soared; in short order nearly all producers copied Laemmle's example. Mary Pickford and Charlie Chaplin, the two most popular players, were able to demand and receive salaries of over $500,000 a year.

The formulas for successful pictures were set fairly early. Westerns were popular, and the big stars were Broncho Billy, Tom Mix and William S. Hart. The theme of crime was repeatedly exploited after *The Great Train Robbery* appeared. Slapstick comedy in its most extravagent versions featured John Bunny, "Fatty" Arbuckle and Mack Sennett's Keystone Cops; Charlie Chaplin created a more sensitive variation on this theme. After Theda Bara's triumph as the vampire (or "vamp") in *A Fool There Was*, sex appeal became a hardy movie perennial. The sentimental story, featuring a child or an animal, was common. And the appearance of extravaganzas such as *Quo Vadis?* testified

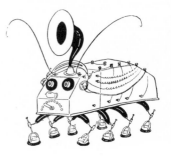

In 1916, when young David Sarnoff concocted a scheme for a radio in every home, he was considered a dreamer. But in less than a decade the whole country had caught the radio bug (above). The early listener had his difficulties, though: Gluyas Williams' cartoon (below) combined several of them in a portrait of frustration which he aptly entitled "Perfect Interference."

to early recognition of the maxim later made famous by Cecil B. DeMille: A religious picture never fails.

By the beginning of the '20s, almost all the distinctive techniques of the films had been devised by David Wark Griffith, a newspaperman, actor and frustrated playwright from Kentucky, so ashamed at first of his movie work that he used a pseudonym for several years. Directing his two greatest films, *The Birth of a Nation* and *Intolerance*, he showed how camera shots could be composed into something different from stage scenes; how, by means of the extreme long shot, the close-up and the pan, or actual movement, the camera itself could participate in the drama; and how light and shadow and symbol could be employed. The great directors who followed Griffith were able to add relatively little in camera technique to what he had originated.

The 1920s saw film making reach its height. The pioneer companies and some new organizations like United Artists, Metro-Goldwyn-Mayer and Warner Brothers became corporations whose assets totaled hundreds of millions. The kind of career possible in movie business was best illustrated by Lewis Selznick. When he decided to give up his small jewelry store, he went job hunting at Universal's offices at a moment when Laemmle was feuding with his partners. To avoid process servers, Laemmle had barricaded himself in an inner sanctum. Selznick saw an opportunity. "If they didn't know what they wanted," he commented later, "I knew what I was after, so I appointed myself to a job, picked out a nice office and went in and took it." Styling himself general manager, he supervised the studios. Each faction assumed the other had appointed him; while they wrangled, he learned the business. By the time he was fired, he knew enough to become a power in the industry.

Producers might be colorful and rich, but they were overshadowed in public acclaim by their stars. The reigning favorites like Mary Pickford, Rudolph Valentino, John Gilbert, Douglas Fairbanks, Harold Lloyd, Pola Negri, Gloria Swanson and Greta Garbo had talent, charm, good looks, or all three. They were part of a society with an exciting reputation for wickedness—a reputation suddenly enhanced in the early '20s. In rapid succession Mary Pickford divorced her first husband to marry Douglas Fairbanks; "Fatty" Arbuckle was charged with manslaughter of a girl; William Deane Taylor, a director, was murdered; and some actors and actresses were exposed as narcotics addicts.

Producers and distributors hastily banded together to enforce morality among their employees and create standards for acceptable films. Former Postmaster General Will Hays was induced to become censor for the film world. The worst scandals died down. But Hollywood, the Los Angeles suburb whose name had become synonymous with the industry, retained its reputation as a place of sin—a stigma that seemed not to affect the earning power of the stars: William S. Hart made $2,225,000 in two years—enough, in an age of business, to qualify as a hero.

THERE was another industry that added significantly to the gross national product in the '20s, raised some men from rags to riches and, in its own way, touched the lives of millions. This was bootlegging. When the prohibition amendment and the Volstead Act went into effect in 1920, making wartime prohibition permanent, nearly everyone assumed they would dry up the country, for Americans had usually observed their laws. In almost no time, however, it became clear that a large part of the public would defy prohibition.

William S. Hart was the top star of Hollywood westerns for 10 years after 1914. Most earlier cowboy movies had been fanciful Wild West shows put on film. But Hart, who had grown up out West, knew what an authentic cowboy was like; he brought to the silent screen a full measure of "two-gun realism."

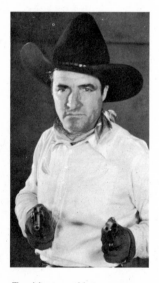

Tom Mix, an athletic young man with a flair for showmanship, insured his success as a cowboy star by buying Tony, a horse which he said had "a genius for acting." Before he and Tony retired in the early '30s, Mix had made nearly 400 films and four million dollars —a tidy profit on a $12.50 horse.

Few Federal Prohibition Bureau investigation agents proved efficient. In New York Izzy Einstein and Moe Smith, a pair of short, fat and able investigators, used an incredible variety of disguises to detect and bring to justice 4,392 offenders. Most agents, however, were not Izzies or Moes. Many were incompetent. Some were both incompetent and overzealous. They used guns so freely as to become terrors of their communities.

Many agents were corrupt. During the first 11 years of prohibition, roughly one in 12 had to be dismissed for cause. Even if they had all been paragons of virtue, there would not have been enough agents. As Fiorello La Guardia said about New York City, enforcing the Volstead Act would require 250,000 police plus another 200,000 to police the policemen.

Within a short time, garages and cellars were turned into private breweries; bathtubs became mixing vats for gin. Saloons reappeared as speakeasies, usually in clandestine locations with peephole doors, but often with a minimum of camouflage. In city, town and hamlet, men on the make turned bootlegger. They hunted up, bought and sold inventories of liquor left over from happier times. They made deals for liquor legally drawn from government warehouses by doctors or druggists, or for moonshine from every corner of the nation. Anything that had a kick was in demand, for customers would pay up to 10 times what they had paid before prohibition for items called Panther Whiskey, Scat Whiskey, Sweet Whiskey and Yack Yack Bourbon—flavored respectively with fusel oil, acetate of lead, ether and iodine.

Clara Bow, the "It" girl of the Jazz Age, declared, "My father is the only person I care for, really." But she had an appeal so rare that, according to one writer, only three others in Hollywood possessed it: Rex the wild stallion, the Latin lover Tony Moreno and the doorman at the Ambassador Hotel.

THE situation offered obvious opportunities for large-scale profits. George Remus of Cincinnati bought up a number of distilleries and warehouses. Protected by bribes to powerful politicians, he sold their inventories, earning an income of over a million dollars a year. Others undertook to supply the mounting demand by wholesale smuggling; ships loaded with booze legitimately purchased in the West Indies lined up on "Rum Row," the international waters just beyond the three-mile limit off the New York and New Jersey coasts. At first rumrunning was a matter of individual enterprise, as with Bill McCoy, the skipper who promised buyers "the real McCoy." But smuggling soon became large-scale and systematic. William Vincent "Big Bill" Dwyer owned a dozen ships and a fleet of speedboats and trucks whose freedom of movement he ensured by regularly paid bribes to a number of policemen, prohibition agents and Coast Guardsmen.

The greatest profits, however, were not in manufacture or importation, but in distribution. Any alcoholic product could be cut, diluted and bottled or rebottled so as to yield a profit of several hundred per cent. If a distributor could establish sufficient control over a district so that bootleggers and speakeasies in it had to buy his merchandise or do without, he could coin money. Obviously contracts concerning the sale of liquor could not be enforced in the courts. So gamblers and panderers, who knew all the tricks of getting police protection, of operating undercover and of making men live up to promises without assistance of the law, were quick to take up the new trade.

In New York gangsters carved up the five boroughs into spheres of interest. Arthur Flegenheimer, better known as Dutch Schultz, was the beer baron of the Bronx. Francesco Uale, racket and liquor boss of Brooklyn, rechristened himself Frankie Yale and, to add to his Ivy League aura, owned a place called the Harvard Inn. After Yale's demise in 1928, the borough of churches passed

The ghost of Michelangelo mesmerizes D. W. Griffith (above), director of "The Birth of a Nation" and the developer of many stars. In 1922 Dorothy Parker wrote of him: "He it was who made, they say, / Movies what they are today; / This the goal for which he's tried —/ Lord, I hope he's satisfied!"

Walt Disney's Mickey Mouse arrived on the screen in 1928 as the hero of "Steamboat Willie." The scrappy rodent was an immediate hit. The League of Nations endorsed him, the Encyclopaedia Britannica wrote him up—and the Russians were so pleased that they called him a proletarian symbol.

to Little Augie Carfano. In Manhattan, Harlem to 42nd Street was the territory of Frankie Marlow until, after a dispute, Carfano had him killed.

The arrangements were shadowy and shifting. There is some evidence that in the early '20s the chief money man of underworld operations was Arnold Rothstein, a handsome, chalk-faced gambler who was rumored to carry with him $100,000 in cash. Rothstein was described by Damon Runyon as "The Brain," by historian Lloyd Morris as "the Morgan of the underworld." At the very least, Rothstein put up money for bootleggers, backed some of the outlets for liquor and financed Jack "Legs" Diamond, who ran the trucks that brought the booze that slaked the thirst of parched New Yorkers. Diamond also used sawed-off shotguns to keep would-be competitors under control. Rothstein was shot to death in 1928. But even before his death, power in New York over liquor, bookmaking, dope and a dozen other such enterprises, was in the hands of a group made up of Charles "Lucky" Luciano, Louis "Lepke" Buchalter, Dandy Phil Kastel, Meyer Lansky, Waxey Gordon, Longy Zwillman and, at the apex, Frank Costello, that cold, quiet, abstemious man, once chief of staff for Big Bill Dwyer.

As early as 1929 Costello, it is said, summoned a conference on the East Coast to which chieftains of crime came from as far away as Chicago. But at first New York was merely one center of bootlegging and allied crimes; its mobs had their counterparts in Detroit's Purple Gang, St. Louis' Egan's Rats, and in Chicago's organization headed by Scarface Al Capone, the Ford or Insull of the bootlegging industry.

I N Chicago the same underworld elements active elsewhere had been quick to take over the illicit liquor trade. Within months after the passage of the Volstead Act, Johnny Torrio, onetime lieutenant of Frankie Yale, asked Yale to come to Chicago and do him a favor. Yale obliged by shooting down Torrio's boss, Big Jim Colosimo. Using Colosimo's organization of hoodlums, policemen and politicians, Torrio quickly gained control over Cook County's breweries and distilleries. He kept some districts in the Windy City for himself and arranged for the distribution of power in the other areas.

Dion O'Banion, an ex-altar boy turned bank robber, got the North Side; a group including the six Genna brothers—the Terrible Gennas—ruled on the West Side; another group, including Polack Joe Saltis and sawed-off-shotgun expert Frank McErlane, had part of the South Side. As his chief enforcer, Torrio imported Capone, who had learned his trade with Frankie Yale.

Torrio's rule did not go unchallenged. In the course of one revolt, O'Banion tipped off prohibition agents, and Torrio was caught shipping beer from a warehouse. Torrio's boys struck back. O'Banion made his headquarters at a flower shop on North State Street. One day three men entered the store, and O'Banion, apparently recognizing them, smiled and reached forward to shake hands. They shot him six times. O'Banion's successor, Hymie Weiss, swore vengeance; Torrio himself was wounded. Though he recovered, he decided that the time had come to retire, and in 1925, nearing the age of 45, he sold his holdings to Capone and left for Italy.

The new boss, Capone, already had his own stronghold. In 1923 he had received from Torrio a franchise for the industrial suburb of Cicero. During city elections the next year, Capone brought in 200 gunmen to see to it that his hand-picked candidates won. Thereafter Cicero was his feudal domain, and it was wide open. Capone used it as a rest-and-recreation center for all the Chicago underworld. His own men walked about, openly armed, and Cicero's mayor, city council and police force did his bidding. Once, when displeased, Capone shoved the mayor down the steps of the city hall and kicked him when he tried to rise. On another occasion he had a recalcitrant councilman bludgeoned in the midst of a council meeting. Once in a while enemy raiding parties reached him. Eleven cars of Weiss gunmen arrived one day and machine-gunned his headquarters, the Hawthorne Hotel. In general, however, Capone was safe in Cicero.

ONE by one, Capone's rivals died violent deaths. Hundreds of men were killed. Weiss was shot down; Schemer Drucci took over his interests; Drucci was killed and was succeeded by Bugs Moran. On February 14, 1929, six of Moran's men and one bystander were trapped in a garage on North Clark Street by five men, three of whom were dressed as policemen. Lined up against a wall, all seven were machine-gunned in the Saint Valentine's Day massacre.

Although Moran escaped and Capone never was able to eliminate all of his rivals in Cook County, Capone, "the big fellow," had clearly made himself more powerful than any of the others. It was an open secret that his power extended into municipal government in the city and most of its suburbs and into the municipal and state courts.

Capone became a tourist attraction. His seven-ton bullet-proof limousine, preceded and followed by cars of bodyguards, was one of the city's sights. When he attended the Sharkey-Stribling fight in Miami Beach, he was escorted to a special seat in the press section. Former world champion Jack Dempsey welcomed him and dusted off his chair. After the fight Capone posed for newsreel cameramen arm in arm with the winner, Sharkey, and former All-American Bill Cunningham. Large numbers of people evidently accepted his own valuation of his trade: "I call myself a businessman," he said, "I make my money by supplying a popular demand. If I break the law, my customers are as guilty as I am."

But Capone had overreached himself. After the Saint Valentine's Day massacre, the Chicago Crime Commission and another investigating body which had dug up evidence on gang murders labeled Capone "Public Enemy Number One" to focus attention on his every action and to stimulate prosecution on any possible ground. Meanwhile Frank Costello called his meeting at Atlantic City where, if rumor is to be believed, he knocked together the heads of Capone and his rivals and told them to behave or else. Returning from this conference, Capone himself was arrested in Philadelphia for carrying a concealed weapon and sentenced to a year in prison.

His stay in Pennsylvania's Eastern Penitentiary was comfortable; he had a cell with two easy chairs, a radio, a bookcase, a rug on the floor and other hotel amenities. When he left, after only 10 months, it was in the warden's car. His return performance in Chicago lasted only for a year, for he was hounded out by publicity. He talked, like Torrio, of getting out—and might have succeeded in ending his successful business career with luxurious retirement. But the federal government tried him for income-tax evasion. Convicted and sentenced, he went to Atlanta and then Alcatraz. His day was over, but he had been a mighty man in his time.

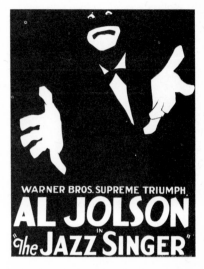

"The Jazz Singer," first feature film with synchronized music and dialogue, appeared in 1927 starring Al Jolson (above). At that time movie producers considered sound a passing fad. But by 1929 silent movies were rapidly vanishing, and theater attendance had almost doubled—to 5.7 billion a year.

The revolt of the dissenters

THE "pointless slaughter" of the war, and a feeling that Wilsonian ideals and the progressive spirit had failed, made the postwar decade a period of revolt, alienation and exile for American intellectuals. Impassioned reformers who had sought to correct economic and social abuses gave way to hostile critics who assailed the manners, mores and institutions of the American majority. With the publication of Sinclair Lewis' *Main Street* in 1920 and *Babbitt* two years later, the empty materialism, corruption and dogmatism of small-town life in mid-America received a savage portrayal. The "civilized" few launched a massive assault upon the philistines, "boobs" and boosters of the new prosperity. To this group politics was vulgar, religion a refuge for the unenlightened, business boorish, and culture nonexistent beyond the Eastern seaboard. *The Nation, The New Republic* and H. L. Mencken's *American Mercury* provided the intellectuals with the platforms from which the "booboisie" could be berated in its money-lined wilderness. Many of the intelligentsia agreed with Mencken that if democracy possessed any merit, "it is the merit . . . of being continuously amusing, of offering the plain people a ribald and endless show." Although the dissenters won few of their day-to-day skirmishes with society, the cumulative effect of their criticism produced lasting changes.

A gathering of Midwestern citizens, banners ready, reflects the provincialism abhorred by intellectuals.

SINCLAIR LEWIS, the first American to win the Nobel Prize for Literature, poses in front of a photo of Sauk Centre, Minnesota, the town he dissected in his novel *Main Street.*

A literary assault on
the religion of the people

DESPITE the 20th Century challenge of secularism and religious modernism, the enthusiastic legions in the ranks of Fundamentalism—the back-to-the-Bible religionists—became more militant than ever, spurred on by the supercharged antics of preachers like Billy Sunday and Aimee Semple McPherson. Sunday, the "Untired Business Man of theology," informed millions of listeners: "Jesus was no dough-faced lick-spittle proposition. Jesus was the greatest scrapper that ever lived." And Sister Aimee, "the world's most pulchritudinous

A familiar country ceremony is shown in John Steuart Curry's painting "Baptism in Kansas." Such rituals riled Sinclair Lewis, but he made i

evangelist," intoxicated her rapt Los Angeles flock at the gaudy Angelus Temple with a carnival of lights, howling sirens, picturesque robes and redemptive exhortations. Sinclair Lewis' *Elmer Gantry*, a "savage caricature of a lecherous charlatan in a ministerial collar," was widely believed to be a take-off on Billy, who had become a millionaire, and Aimee, who was rumored to have a lover. Its publication and Lewis' public challenge to God to strike him dead made him a prime spokesman for those who were repelled by popular religion in their country.

clear that he was attacking all organized religion, not just the Baptists.

The "preacher novel" satirizes pious sham.

Billy Sunday blasts sinners from the pulpit.

Sister Aimee preaches at Angelus Temple.

MEMBERS' FERVOR, seen in these cartoons, is reflected in Rotary's growth during the '20s to 3,000 clubs in 44 countries. There were also 1,200 Lions Clubs, and 1,800 Kiwanis. Mencken acidly described Rotary as "organized lovey-dovey," designed to convince men "that its puerile mumbo-jumbo can convert stock-brokers . . . into passable imitations of Francis Xavier."

A snarling elite opposed to businessmen joiners

To wryly observant cynics, the noisy weekly luncheons of the businessmen's service clubs, with their chummy sentimentality and mystical belief in the "regenerative influence of business" had the "tinkle of coin in it." Writers of the period pointed out that the lines between religion and business had begun to blur; for they found little difference between the speaker who called Rotary "a manifestation of the divine" and the churchmen who were offering "preferred capital stock in the Kingdom of God" and "salvation and five per cent." What critics of the vulgarization of religion and the exaltation of business failed to perceive was that the antidemocratic order championed by Mencken was just as dangerous to American ideals as were the manifestations of ignorance that drew his unremitting wrath.

SURROUNDED by spectators and reporters, Mencken is seen before being led off to a Boston jail for selling a copy of *The American Mercury* which ran a short story about a prostitute.

A Chicago Rotary Thanksgiving lunch in 1922 adds an exotic flavor by honoring Scottish entertainer Sir Harry Lauder (center, in kilts).

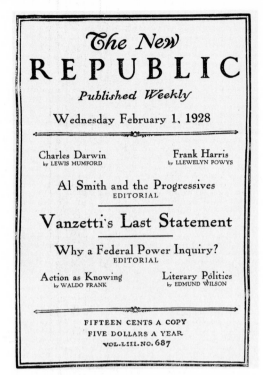

The New
REPUBLIC
Published Weekly

Wednesday February 1, 1928

Charles Darwin
by LEWIS MUMFORD

Frank Harris
by LLEWELYN POWYS

Al Smith and the Progressives
EDITORIAL

Vanzetti's Last Statement

Why a Federal Power Inquiry?
EDITORIAL

Action as Knowing
by WALDO FRANK

Literary Politics
by EDMUND WILSON

FIFTEEN CENTS A COPY
FIVE DOLLARS A YEAR
VOL. LIII. NO. 687

VOICING DISSENT on a wide variety of topics, this single issue of *The New Republic* deals with science, literature, philosophy, government and politics.

A decade's conscience in the hands of the few

CONCERN about the political and social problems of the '20s was most strongly voiced by those members of the intellectual community who contributed to certain small-circulation magazines. In issue after issue of these politically oriented journals, articulate liberals wrote impassioned protests against the scandals and corruptions of the decade. One of the most important of these publications was *The New Republic (left)*. Although its circulation was dwindling during these years, the magazine continued to speak out forcefully on subjects ranging from the ominous growth of the K.K.K. *(right)* to the "fifteen men in a smoke-filled room" kind of sordid politics that nominated Warren G. Harding *(below)*. The magazine's offices became a headquarters for dissenters of every persuasion—poets, workers from Chicago's Hull-House, maverick Junior Leaguers and Bryn Mawr graduates. And all spoke loudly enough to justify the belief of Herbert Croly, its editor, that "Even an insignificant weekly can . . . keep faith alive. . . ."

PICKING A CANDIDATE at 1 a.m. in the original "smoke-filled room" in Chicago, Republican chiefs decide to run Harding for President in 1920. This act became a symbol for boss control.

INITIATION OF A KLANSMAN features a flaming cross, visible for miles and symbolic of the Ku Klux Klan's violence. The red-robed figure is called the Great Titan, a regional officer.

The lure of life abroad as an antidote to provincialism

For those who had the fare, self-exile seemed to promise a "more satisfying intellectual life than there is at home." At least 85 American writers lived in Europe between 1915 and 1930, mostly in France; some like Ernest Hemingway *(left)* produced important works while abroad. But one critic noted that many expatriates railed "against American grossness and American puritanism in one breath and as if they were the same thing."

For many American expatriates, their country's provincialism was epitomized by the yearly "Chautauqua Week"—a traveling tent carnival of "music, drama, magic, art lessons, cooking classes, low comedy and high-minded debates" that brought both entertainment and education to countless towns otherwise cut off from cultural sources. The self-exiled had rejected the restrictions of small-town America, but the scene change had not always supplied a magical answer. Gertrude Stein, *doyenne* of the Americans in Paris, commented to Hemingway, her young protégé: "You are all a lost generation."

An Iowa harvesting crew eats a noonday meal in Grant Wood's "Dinner for Threshers." Many expatriates came out of the Midwest, and a

CULTURE AT HOME is seen in this Grant Wood drawing, "O, Chautauqua!" Eminent politicians and aspiring candidates of both major parties rode the circuit, along with dazzling virtuosos like Montaville Flowers, who recited all the parts in *Ben-Hur.*

European avant-garde magazine, "transatlantic review," reported that most of its English-language manuscripts "came from west of Altoona."

CRUSADER Margaret Sanger leaves a courthouse after a conviction for providing contraception information at her birth-control center.

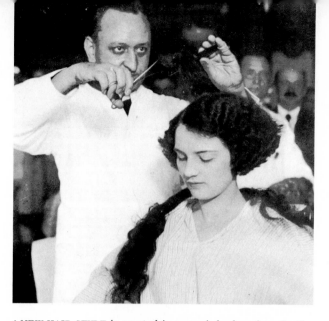

A NEW HAIR STYLE is created in a men's barber shop. In the early '20s bobbed hair was anathema to protectors of the old order and was associated with radicalism and even "free love."

The fight of the women against the Victorian code

Among the shock troops of the "antipuritan revolt" were the daughters of the American middle class. Having shown during the war that women were as capable as men in the workaday world, and having won the right to vote, women now demanded full social equality as well. Many symbolic hobbles of the prewar woman were discarded. Dresses were shortened, hair was cut, billowy bathing ensembles gave way to snug, more revealing, one-piece suits. The writings of Freud and Havelock Ellis, often distorted by popularizers, stimulated an almost obsessive concern with sex. One of the most devastating blows to the sensibilities of the guardians of public morality was struck by Margaret Sanger (above). As a nurse in New York's tenement districts, she had seen chronic anguish among families who tried to raise too many children on too little income. Distressed, she agitated for birth control. Disregarding setbacks, including a jail term, she lived to see some 200 Planned Parenthood clinics opened throughout the U.S.

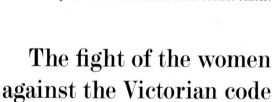

A STRUGGLING BATHER is a problem for the harassed man trying to put her into a Chicago paddy wagon in 1922. Special policewomen usually made these seaside arrests.

A NEW ESCAPE from established rules is shown in this movie scene. Hollywood both stimulated and reported the fads and fancies of the public, and films often showed how the automobile was used by young people to escape the supervision of parents. The car was attacked as a wicked "room . . . which could be . . . moved at will into a darkened byway or a country lane."

ABUSE of power in business and in politics is the target of the exposé *Oil!*, the novel that is shown above.

Under attack: corruption and the high life

The documented attack on corruption, made popular by the muckrakers, aroused very little public interest in the '20s. However in 1927 Upton Sinclair published *Oil!*, an account of the roughshod tactics of the oil industry and a slashing indictment of the scandalous bribery of public officials during Harding's Administration. Although the book was fictional, readers could identify real people, such as William Randolph Hearst, then the most powerful newspaper publisher in the U.S., and his estate at San Simeon, one of whose rooms is seen at right. Called "The Monastery" in the novel, this $30 million complex of ornate temples and castles was stuffed with art treasures. To Sinclair, the most infuriating aspect of Hearst's imperial way of life was that the publisher openly defied all moral codes and got away with it.

5. THE
JAZZ AGE

PUBLIC adulation of the automobile and utility magnates, movie stars and bootleggers, who were the heroes of the '20s, emphasized individual success stories. For the nation, however, there was far more significance in the impact on American life of the business activities of these celebrities. The auto, for example, changed middle-class American life more than any other invention or device except the building of the railroads. In their book *Middletown* (a pseudonym for Muncie, Indiana), the classic study of the mores of a small Midwestern city in the mid-1920s, Robert and Helen Lynd listed some of the effects of the motorcar. Housewives could leave home in the daytime to shop and enjoy themselves. Families that never previously thought of taking a vacation now toured for two weeks in the summer. Some, previously devout, became lax in church attendance in order to take Sunday drives.

Use of the family automobile was an important source of conflict between teenagers and their parents. For high school youngsters the automobile also changed courtship patterns and morals. Said the Lynds: ". . . in 1890 a 'well-brought-up' boy and girl were commonly forbidden to sit together in the dark. . . . In an auto, however, a party may go to a city halfway across the state in an afternoon or evening, and unchaperoned automobile parties as late as midnight, while subject to criticism, are not exceptional."

The impact of electricity was somewhat different. Housewives who could afford them bought vacuum cleaners, washing machines, refrigerators, better

A SINGER OF SPIRITUALS, Ruby Green is luminously portrayed in James Chapin's painting. She was one of many Negro performers who gained recognition in the '20s.

irons and sewing machines. The combination of trucking and electric refrigeration made possible good neighborhood grocery stores, reducing the necessity for canning, preserving and other home chores. Similarly, electrified commercial laundries cut down the amount of scrubbing, starching and ironing that needed to be done, all of which added significantly to leisure time.

Movies and speakeasies were two of the places in which the emancipated householders could spend this free time. By the end of the '20s weekly attendance at movies was estimated at 110 million. Movie theaters had come a long way from the peep-show and nickelodeon days. Many were now substantial buildings—in small places sometimes the most sumptuous structure in town, in cities often deserving their new designation as movie palaces.

For some, going to a movie was, as a *Saturday Evening Post* ad said, "If only for an afternoon or an evening—escape!" For others it was an education. Ernst Lubitsch, the famous German movie director, studied American pictures before starting work in Hollywood and observed that American audiences were most interested in learning such things as which fork to use.

The early five-cent movies had been aimed at workingmen; the 25-cent-to-two-dollar films of the '20s were directed at the growing white-collar class—the people most eager to learn how the well-to-do lived. Hundreds of postwar films presented the Hollywood version of a high society in which the hip flask, the fast car and the casual affair were the correct thing. Movies reported quickly, and to some extent accurately, on wealthy young women, the "flappers," who bobbed their hair, wore short skirts, used lipstick, smoked cigarettes and drank cocktails. In short order, flapper styles were the rage; the cosmetics industry boomed, cigarette sales increased enormously, high heels decorated brass rails of speakeasy bars from Bangor to San Diego.

The torch singer of her generation, Helen Morgan, led a tragic life. At the peak of her career in the '20s she earned $3,500 a week, but she died a penniless alcoholic. A columnist wrote sadly: "She had in her voice the note of heartbreak—authentic heartbreak, worth its weight in theater gold."

JUST how much of the new leisure time was spent in speakeasies is hard to say. The speakeasies were less numerous than pre-prohibition saloons, and the probability is that there were fewer drinkers in the '20s than before. But the speakeasy served a different purpose. The saloons in working-class neighborhoods were, with certain notable exceptions, run-down establishments where the booze was bad, and the free lunch worse and the bartender doubled as a pander and gambler's tout. The saloon had, however, served as a workingman's club. The typical speakeasy, on the other hand, was patronized, as was the bootlegger, by the white-collar worker, the college student with a good allowance, or the men and women who before prohibition would have done their drinking mainly at home, at private parties or private clubs.

The most elegant speakeasies quickly assumed the role of romantic rendezvous. Going to a speakeasy became fashionable, especially if it had a few jazz musicians and if a celebrity—the more notorious the better—made it his hangout. It was equally fashionable to get thoroughly drunk.

Obviously, there were great numbers of Americans who did not spend their leisure time in speakeasies or movies. Across the country, book and magazine sales were up 40 to 50 per cent. Public libraries, museums, art and music classes increased. Incalculable hours were given to listening to phonograph records and radio programs. The first commercial radio broadcast was transmitted by Pittsburgh station KDKA in November 1920, and many other stations soon went on the air. By the mid-'20s home radio receivers were common and loudspeakers had replaced earphones; people listened to music, sports-

"A ranch near Waco, Texas, a sucker town," produced Texas Guinan, mistress of Broadway's night life during the wildest years of prohibition. Her speakeasies were forever being raided, and though she denied it, she was reported to have punned by greeting her lawyer with "Hello, succor."

casts, news reports, special programs (such as political conventions), comedy skits and, of course, sponsors' messages.

Measured simply in terms of the vast number of hours of leisure time consumed, sports in the '20s became a paramount interest of the American people. The numbers of golfers, tennis players, bowlers and amateur baseball players increased phenomenally. In 1920, there were fewer than 2,000 golf courses in the country; the number more than tripled by 1930. Bowling teams increased from 5,000 in 1920 to more than 40,000 in 1930.

Attendance at baseball, football and basketball games, boxing and wrestling matches and horse races set new marks all through the '20s. Promoter Tex Rickard learned how to draw genteel crowds to prize fights. In 1921 he pitted heavyweight champion Jack Dempsey against Georges Carpentier, a slightly built French war hero. The fight took place in Jersey City on July 2, in a clean, well-run arena and it produced the first million-dollar gate. Millions of people outside the arena followed this and subsequent title matches by radio or saw the newsreels. In 1926, when Dempsey lost his title to Gene Tunney, 120,000 fans paid $1.8 million to see the dethroning. And the second Dempsey-Tunney fight, in 1927, drew an all-time record $2,658,660. Dempsey floored his opponent but was slow in returning to a neutral corner. Tunney thereby got extra seconds of grace before the "long count" began and was able to recover and keep the title he had won a year before.

The '20s were the golden years of baseball. People who had never seen the inside of a major-league stadium anguished over the "Black Sox" scandal, when eight Chicago White Sox players took money to throw the 1919 World Series, a shocking incident that brought about the appointment of Judge Kenesaw M. Landis as "czar" of organized baseball.

Tens of millions followed the career of George Herman "Babe" Ruth, a homely slum kid from Baltimore with a giant's torso, spindly legs and dainty feet. In 22 years in the major leagues, the Babe set many records, a number of which still stood 25 years after he left the game. He hit more home runs (714) than anyone ever had. In 1927 he slammed 60 home runs to set the record for a 154-game season. The Babe's slugging feats were memorable: On one unforgettable day in the World Series of 1932, he pointed his finger at a spot in the center-field bleachers and, on the next pitch, sent the ball rocketing precisely to that spot. When Ruth was chided about the fact that his $80,000 salary was higher than President Hoover's, he is supposed to have observed, after a moment's meditation, "Well, I had a better year."

Among the spectator sports, football and basketball also attracted tremendous crowds. In 1930 total attendance at college football games was more than 10 million, and gate receipts were at least $20 million. Basketball games, mainly between high schools, drew so many fans that in the mid-'20s people talked of a "basketball craze."

Idol Rudolph Valentino longed for the farm life he had left in Italy, and he spent his leisure time discussing art, singing folk songs and cooking spaghetti. When a story called him "Rudy, the beautiful gardener's boy," he was furious and challenged the writer to a fist fight. The writer declined.

Nearly all sports enjoyed new popularity. A crop of superb athletes inspired almost religious devotion by sports fans—Bill Tilden and Helen Wills in tennis; Gertrude Ederle and Johnny Weissmuller in swimming; Walter Hagen, Gene Sarazen and the incomparable Bobby Jones in golf; Barney Oldfield and the Englishman Malcolm Campbell in auto racing; Willie Hoppe in billiards. The '20s were years when many Americans began turning to the front pages only after reading the sports section.

When Charles Lindbergh (above) landed in Paris, his feat set off jubilation amazing even in that exuberant era. Almost immediately, ukuleles were twanging "Lucky Lindy" (below), a song whose words glorified the heroic young aviator: "Just like a child he simply smiled / While we were wild with fear."

The enormous popularity of sports was part and parcel of a widespread hankering after sensations that characterized the Harding-Coolidge era. Astrology flourished. For a while, Émile Coué's autosuggestion was the rage— practitioners repeated to themselves, "Every day in every way I am getting better and better." This fad was succeeded by mah-jongg, crossword puzzles, bridge. New forms of music gained popularity—the crooners' melodies of Rudy Vallee, the blues, the torch song and especially jazz. The bawl of the saxophone was as characteristic of the period as the blare of the automobile horn.

New dances came in and the established fox trot had to share popularity with the Charleston and the Black Bottom. There were the degrading spectacles of marathon dance contests in which couples, competing for a prize, clung to one another, dancing for days with only brief respite until one pair outlasted all the others.

THE hunger for new thrills was most apparent in what was read. Bernarr Macfadden's *True Story* magazine, started in 1919, had almost two million subscribers by 1926. Other sex and confession magazines, featuring stories such as "The Primitive Lover," "Indolent Kisses" and "What I Told My Daughter the Night before Her Marriage," enjoyed similar success. The tabloid New York *Daily News*, also launched in 1919, attained the highest daily circulation in America five years after it started publication. Soon a number of cities had similar papers in which pictures and big headlines predominated and the lead stories usually had to do with either sex or crime.

Back in 1892 Miss Lizzie Borden of Fall River, Massachusetts, in the words of a contemporary jingle, "took an ax and gave her mother forty whacks; when she saw what she had done, she gave her father forty-one!" Newspapers had reported her trial with relative restraint. But in the '20s, covering the equally horrendous Leopold-Loeb and Hall-Mills murders, the papers gave so much space to the trials that for weeks there was little room on the front page for any other stories.

Richard Loeb and Nathan Leopold Jr., two brilliant and precocious teenage sons of prominent and wealthy Chicago families, were arrested and charged with kidnaping and killing 14-year-old Bobby Franks on May 21, 1924, and then demanding ransom from his father. After first denying the charges, they calmly confessed. They had done it, they said, mainly for the thrill of committing a perfect crime.

In July they were tried. Clarence Darrow, the great defense lawyer who hated capital punishment, represented them. Their plea was guilty, and there was no jury, for the only issue was whether the sentence should be imprisonment or death. For 33 days the state's attorney and Darrow battled while the nation's press reported the clashes in detail. "Why did they kill little Bobby Franks?" asked Darrow: "Not for money, not for spite, not for hate. They killed him as they might kill a spider or a fly, for the experience. They killed him because they were made that way." Darrow's plea won, and the boys were sentenced to jail for life.

Two years after the Leopold-Loeb trial, Mrs. Frances Stevens Hall was put on trial in New Jersey for the murder of her husband, the Reverend Edward W. Hall, and his mistress, Mrs. James Mills. The proceedings were full of drama. One desperately ill witness was carried into court on a bed to testify for the prosecution. Hour after hour, the state's attorney read aloud from the love letters that the parson had written his inamorata—"My own true, darling heart. . ." "What a mad gypsy you were this afternoon . . ." Mrs. Hall was acquitted, but meanwhile, as Bruce Bliven wrote in *The New Republic*, "Journals yellow and journals white wallow[ed] in it." In 20 days the usually restrained and august New York *Times* gave the case 340,000 words.

The most publicized exploit of the '20s, however, had in it no touch of sex or scandal. On May 20, 1927, Captain Charles A. Lindbergh took off from Roosevelt Field, New York, for Paris, flying alone in his single-engine monoplane, the *Spirit of St. Louis*. The whole nation held its breath as he piloted his tiny craft past Newfoundland through fog and rain and sleet, disappeared into the stormy North Atlantic and finally landed safely at Le Bourget airport near Paris. When word came that this first nonstop transatlantic solo flight had been a success, the New York *Times* splashed a headline across eight columns, in type usually reserved for war news: "LINDY DOES IT—TO PARIS IN 33½ HOURS." Lindbergh came home and was given a triumphal parade by New York City: 1,800 tons of confetti fell along the route.

In a way the Lindbergh demonstrations epitomized the tendency among Americans of the '20s to overdo—in celebrations, in scandals, in sports, in moviegoing, in drinking bathtub gin. For a sizable part of the population, it was an age of excess.

Fierce-tempered Ty Cobb (above), who once jumped into the stands and attacked a fan, had a phenomenal lifetime batting average through 1928 of .367; in 1911 he batted .420. In his first professional game, he hit a home run and a double but was dismissed from the team for "lack of ability."

THE gaiety with which nostalgia later adorned the '20s passed unnoticed by most Negroes. Especially in Northern cities, Negro leaders (whose people made up a tenth of the nation's population) pointed more and more vigorously to the paradox of the economic and social plight of their race in the midst of boom times. Valiantly but with little success the National Association for the Advancement of Colored People and the Commission on Interracial Cooperation fought for the Negro's right to vote and pressed the case for federal antilynching legislation.

Despairing of any remedy within the existing system, hundreds of thousands of Negroes listened to the message of Marcus Garvey, whose Universal Negro Improvement Association stood for black superiority and agitated for wholesale return to Africa and the creation there of a black empire. Garvey, a West Indian, was a powerful personality, with more imagination than business skill, who raised some $10 million in two years but fell afoul of the postal authorities in 1925 and went to prison for using the mails to defraud. The collapse of his movement—the first mass movement of American Negroes—intensified the drive for a solution to the Negro's problems through persistent agitation within the United States.

There was, during this time, an intellectual renaissance within the Negro community that brought recognition by white audiences of talented Negro actors and songwriters. Negro poets and novelists like Claude McKay, Langston Hughes, James Weldon Johnson and Walter White attracted the favorable attention of avant-garde literary circles. But these limited achievements merely served to mask the increasing seriousness of the Negro problem.

There were millions of others who also went untouched by the boom. By 1929 the average production worker in manufacturing made only five cents more per hour than he had in 1921. Many companies had waged successful battles against unions, and AFL membership shrank from over four million in 1920 to under three million in 1929.

"Little Miss Poker Face," Helen Wills, serenely won the U.S. women's tennis championship when she was only 17. Her protective sun visor became the latest fashion rage. A visored laborer in Connecticut brained a friend with a shovel when the friend pointed at him and taunted "Helen Wills!"

Blond, blue-eyed Walter White had only a trace of Negro blood, but he insisted on being called a Negro. His Caucasian features allowed him to interview members of lynch mobs, then make damning reports for the N.A.A.C.P. Once the Ku Klux Klan actually sounded him out about working for it.

W.E.B. Du Bois, Harvard's first Negro Ph.D., disagreed with Booker T. Washington's assertion that "there is as much dignity in tilling a field as in writing a poem." Du Bois contended: "We shall hardly induce black men to believe that if their stomachs be full, it matters little about their brains."

In some industries, it is true, the idea gained ground that workers were steadier and more efficient if well treated, and certain companies voluntarily raised wages, reduced hours and offered fringe benefits. But where they had no union to argue their case, workers had to accept the decisions of their employers. Even where unions existed, they were often too weak to win concessions. When steel-company heads refused to negotiate the abandonment of the 12-hour day, steelworkers struck. The strike failed, and workers reconciled themselves to company dictates. For the lower segments of the working class, the '20s were not happy years.

Another large group of discontented Americans was the farmers, experiencing a sharp agricultural depression. Sharing their unhappiness were the merchants and professional men in the small towns of agricultural regions. Brought up to believe that farms and small towns were the backbone of America, all these people found it galling that the cities, reputedly crowded with foreigners and reeking of corruption, were granted a prosperity denied to them. While their common sense led to campaigns for farm legislation, their emotions found other releases.

One was Fundamentalism. Most of rural America was devoutly Protestant, and the church or churches—Methodist or Baptist or, less frequently, Presbyterian, Congregational, Lutheran or Disciples of Christ—formed the only centers, aside from family get-togethers, for social and recreational gatherings. Pastors, preachers, deacons, elders or Sunday school teachers—largely people of little education—were spiritual descendants of those men who in the late 19th Century had vaguely sensed the threat to their old-time religion posed by the new theological speculations called the "social gospel" and the "higher criticism."

The World's Christian Fundamentals Association was organized in 1918. Trumpeting the peril to the faith represented by Darwinism, its journal described the theory of evolution as an attack on the Bible, a challenge to the revealed truth in the Book of Genesis, a denial of man's divine creation.

EARLY in the '20s Fundamentalists launched a campaign to ban the teaching of Darwinism in schools. A bill in Kentucky failed by a single vote; one in Tennessee passed both houses and became law; in more than a dozen other states similar measures were introduced. The Anti-Evolution League, formed in 1924, looked hopefully to the day when the Constitution would be amended by language similar to that in Tennessee's Butler Act, which made it unlawful for anyone in a university or school wholly or partly supported by public funds "to teach any theory that denies the story of the Divine Creation of man as taught in the Bible. . . ."

In 1925 John Thomas Scopes, a quiet high school teacher in Dayton, Tennessee, agreed to let one of his friends, who wanted to test the constitutionality of the law, file suit against him for violating the Butler Act. A noted figure in the Fundamentalist movement, William Jennings Bryan, offered to help the prosecution. The American Civil Liberties Union defended Scopes, and when Bryan entered the case, Clarence Darrow asked to join the defense. The prospect of a confrontation between two such adversaries drew the eyes of the whole nation to Dayton and the issues to be debated there.

Newspapers covered the trial that summer with the same avidity they displayed for the Leopold-Loeb and Hall-Mills cases. The weather was hot.

Bryan and Darrow doffed their coats and argued in shirt sleeves. The home-town crowd was with Bryan; so were the judge and jury. When Darrow tried to put scientists on the stand, the court refused to permit them to testify.

Darrow was nothing, however, if not resourceful. He asked if Bryan would take the stand to testify as an expert on the Bible. Made incautious by his success, Bryan agreed. Darrow then put Bryan through a merciless cross-examination, forcing him to reveal humiliating ignorance and confusion. Nonetheless, the jury found Scopes guilty.

Eventually the Tennessee Supreme Court reversed the decision. More important, the Fundamentalists were discredited in the public mind. Even the genial humorist Will Rogers said Bryan was wrong, "More wrong than he has ever been before. . . . He might make Tennessee the side show of America, but he can't make a street carnival of the whole United States." Only a few days after the trial, Bryan, 65, collapsed and died. Some said it was of a broken heart. Darrow, knowing his opponent's lifelong habit of overeating, muttered uncharitably, "Broken heart nothing; he died of a busted belly."

ANOTHER emotional outlet for rural Americans was the Ku Klux Klan. One night in 1915 William Joseph Simmons, a former Methodist circuit preacher teaching Southern history at little Lanier University in Atlanta, led 15 friends up Stone Mountain; there, beneath a fiery cross, they vowed to re-create this secret society of the Reconstruction era. Under Simmons as Imperial Wizard, there was to be a hierarchy moving downward from Grand Goblins to Grand Dragons, Great Titans and Exalted Cyclopes. "Klonklaves" of local Klan units were to be held according to an elaborate ritual, the individual Knights attiring themselves in white robes and peaked hoods that masked their faces. They spoke a secret language (as, for example, "Akia," meaning "a Klansman I am," to which a reply might be "Kigy," or "Klansman, I greet you").

Although it was dedicated to white supremacy from the outset, the Klan might have remained a crackpot local organization if several forces had not come into play. One was World War I, which had given some Negroes new aspirations, thereby arousing apprehensions among Southern whites. Another was a recruiting campaign launched in 1920 by Edward Young Clarke, an unscrupulous promoter who saw the money-making potential of the K.K.K.

Named Imperial Kleagle, or national membership chairman, Clarke enlisted hundreds of local Kleagles. Each was empowered to sign up as many new members as he could, collecting from each a $10 initiation fee and keeping four dollars for himself. In parts of the country where white supremacy was the principal concern, Kleagles stressed that aspect of the organization's creed. In other localities, where antievolutionism, anti-Catholicism, anti-Semitism or nativism were rife, they could emphasize instead the K.K.K.'s Fundamentalist Protestant character or its 100 per cent Americanism. For four dollars a head, Kleagles worked tirelessly, and by 1922 the Klan had 100,000 Knights.

Some of these recruits were sadists of the worst sort, seeking the shelter of a mask and the comfort of a crowd to give organizational sanction to their brutality. Numerous instances of Klan violence were reported. The press, led by the New York *World* in 1920, published exposés that described the beating of a lawyer in South Carolina, the branding of a bellhop in Dallas, the tarring

In his fine uniform and hat with plumes as "tall as Guinea grass," Marcus Garvey led the Back-to-Africa movement. "Where is the black man's government... ? Where is his president, his country and his ambassador, his army, his navy, his men of big affairs?" he asked. "Up, you mighty race!"

A waltz from the Gay '90s, "The Sidewalks of New York," was revived as Al Smith's campaign song. The popular humor magazine "Life" put its finger on an important issue by distorting a line in the song ("East Side, West Side") into "East Side, Wet's Side," a gibe at Smith's antiprohibitionism.

As a presidential hopeful in 1928, Herbert Hoover aroused no great enthusiasm among Republican senators. They dubbed him "Sir Herbert," a snide rebuke for his stays in England, and they even accused him of robbing a Chinese. In spite of such falsities, Hoover was chosen on the first ballot.

and feathering of an Episcopal archdeacon in Florida, the flogging of a man and woman in Alabama and the drowning of two men in Louisiana.

Surprisingly, and disturbingly, this publicity failed to hurt the Klan. On the contrary, by 1924 its membership had leaped to about four million. Nor was the Klan confined to the South. The largest single concentration was in Indiana, with 500,000 members, but the fiery cross burned in almost every area where there were farms and small towns peopled predominantly by white Anglo-Saxon Protestants.

With expansion came, however, a degree of internal reform. A coup within the Klonvokation forced Simmons out of power and put in his place a Dallas dentist, Hiram Wesley Evans. Evans fired Clarke, ended the fee-splitting practice, rid the Klan of some of its most outrageous members and made certain other changes in procedure. However night rides, beatings, floggings, burnings and killings continued.

The Klan became a power in local and state politics. Avowed Klansmen were elected county officials, legislators and convention delegates. Klan-supported candidates won governorships and seats in Congress. Two United States Senators from Georgia were probably members; the governor of Alabama and a senator from Texas certainly carried membership cards. At the Democratic national convention in 1924, Klan leaders were conspicuously present, lobbying against a proposed platform plank that would have condemned their organization as un-American and campaigning for the nomination of William G. McAdoo over Alfred E. Smith. The plank they opposed was defeated. However, neither McAdoo nor Smith was nominated.

The following year the Invisible Empire, as the Klan styled itself, received some more free publicity. The Grand Dragon for Indiana, David Curtis Stephenson, was a holdover from Simmons' time. In March 1925, a girl in Indianapolis poisoned herself, and before she died accused Stephenson of rape. Stephenson was tried, convicted and sentenced to life imprisonment.

THIS was the turning point. The Klan's membership rolls began to shrink. Its candidates were badly defeated in several states, and in 1927 Alabama's attorney general publicly resigned his membership and began indicting Klansmen for acts of terrorism. By 1928, the four million had melted away to scattered cells of die-hards.

The fears and anxieties of rural America flared up again in 1928, when the Democrats nominated Al Smith for President. One of the ablest and most humane governors in New York history, Smith had surmounted his Tammany Hall background. But his speech pattern, formed during his childhood on New York City's Lower East Side, his brown derby hat and his cigar made him, in rural eyes, the embodiment of the wicked city. To Fundamentalist America, Alfred E. Smith was one of the new men who were threatening to take over their country. As a Roman Catholic and an opponent of prohibition, he was equally suspect.

The Anti-Saloon League rose up, with Methodist Bishop James Cannon Jr. and his adjutants once again in full voice. Fundamentalist associations rallied their parsons to fight the popish menace and, in effect, threatened to excommunicate any who voted for Smith. The remnants of the Klan rose in a fury against Smith. In the Solid South veteran Democrats bolted the ticket and when the votes were added up, Smith had lost five states—Virginia, North Carolina, Florida, Tennessee and Texas. Later on, political analysts were to realize that while losing in the South, Smith had recruited to his party a much larger following among the urban minority groups. In the long view, Smith's campaign had laid the foundation for a new and more powerful Democratic party. But what was most apparent in 1928 was the unhappiness and intolerance of rural white Protestants.

For diametrically opposed reasons, another and much smaller segment was just as unhappy. But the intellectuals who made up this group had an influence far beyond their numbers. Some writers, poets, artists, musicians and philosophers did find the '20s satisfying years. The increase in book reading that came with added leisure meant increases in sales. The number of professional authors grew from 7,000 in 1920 to 12,000 in 1930, and some of these rejoiced with Sinclair Lewis' character, George Babbitt, that "the man who . . . shows both purpose and pep in handling his literary wares has a chance to drag down his fifty thousand bucks a year, to mingle with the biggest executives on terms of perfect equality, and to show as big a house and as swell a car as any Captain of Industry!"

Mr. Babbitt probably would have been an avid reader of *The Man Nobody Knows*, written by a very successful advertising man, Bruce Barton, senior partner in the firm of Batten, Barton, Durstine & Osborn. Barton's bestseller was an assertion of the vulgar thesis that Jesus and His disciples had been go-getting businessmen who staged history's greatest sales campaign.

Any first-rate author, even if his usual vein was cheerful and optimistic, was apt to be critical when commenting on the times. E. E. Cummings, generally a somewhat whimsical poet, published a novel, *The Enormous Room*, in which the central character concluded that life in a prison camp had advantages over life outside.

Intellectuals were rebelling against prudishness, and there was an outpouring of novels and plays that featured earthy scenes and language. Many novelists, playwrights and poets, influenced by the profound studies of Sigmund Freud into the workings of the human mind, were dealing with subjects formerly considered unmentionable. James Branch Cabell's *Jurgen*, for instance, was a long, somewhat monotonous exercise in double meaning. When its plates were seized by the New York Society for the Suppression of Vice, the literary world rose up to defend it as a work of art, as little subject to censorship as any other work of art such as the Bible or Shakespeare. The critics themselves blushed later at their hasty praise, but *Jurgen* remained memorable as a symbol of the intellectuals' reaction to what they scornfully termed puritanism.

WRITERS also rebelled against commercialism and materialism. Living in self-imposed exile, Ezra Pound and T. S. Eliot wrote poems touching this theme. Both were to remain abroad, Pound eventually becoming a propagandist for Mussolini and Eliot taking British citizenship and settling down to staid life as a conservative London editor. Ernest Hemingway, whose style was to influence a whole generation of writers, spent much of this period in France. At home Ellen Glasgow, Willa Cather, Theodore Dreiser and John Dos Passos turned out novels that, in one way or another, pictured America as an intellectually and culturally sterile land dominated by businessmen and business values.

Al Smith carried a heavy load of political liabilities in 1928. In the cartoon above, his burdens include a friar, representing his Catholic faith, and the Tammany tiger. An editor summed up the bitter anti-Smith view: "[Puritan] civilization, which has built a sturdy, orderly nation, is threatened by Smith."

Novelist Sinclair Lewis said that Willa Cather (above) should have received the Nobel Prize conferred on him. Among Miss Cather's admirable qualities, Lewis said, was "the courage to be tender and perfectly simple." The caricatures on these pages were drawn by the noted artist Miguel Covarrubias.

Sportswriter Ring Lardner, who won fame in 1914 for his hilarious baseball satires, was a gloomy, sardonic man. In the '20s, as his fame increased, his despondency deepened. When asked the 10 most beautiful words in the English language, he included "mange," "wretch," "scram" and "gangrene."

One of the archcritics of American life in the '20s was Sinclair Lewis, a tall, gawky, red-haired man with an acne-pitted face, violent temper and inexhaustible energy. He was born in Sauk Centre, Minnesota, a town of less than 3,000. During his youth he had been the butt of town humorists because he lacked the eye and co-ordination to excel at boys' games. As a grown man he recalled Sauk Centre's citizens with a painful mixture of sentimentality and malice. His capacity for recollecting and parodying speech was fantastic. One acquaintance said: "Remembering Lewis, one always felt, after we parted, that there had been a dozen men in the room."

Lewis took his revenge on Sauk Centre by bringing it to life as "Gopher Prairie, Minnesota" in his novel *Main Street*. This was the story of a sensitive and culturally ambitious woman, Carol Kennicott, who was almost stifled by the trivial preoccupations, the dull routine, the banal conversation and the ugliness of the typical small town.

Babbitt, Lewis' second successful novel, was set in a somewhat larger Midwestern town, Zenith. The hero, George Babbitt, a go-getting real estate salesman and member of the Boosters Club, delivered himself of such homilies as: "Trouble with a lot of folks is . . . they don't see the spiritual and mental side of American supremacy; they think that inventions like the telephone . . . are all that we stand for; whereas to a real thinker, he sees that spiritual and, uh, dominating movements like Efficiency, and Rotarianism, and Prohibition, and Democracy are what compose our deepest and truest wealth."

Deep down, Lewis believed in the values of the small town. In his novels he was saying not that the values were wrong but only that Main Street stultified beauty and did not live up to the ideals it proclaimed.

THE other archcritic of American civilization was H. L. Mencken. Mencken was a newspaperman, largely self-educated, who won fame as a master of invective. After some years on the Baltimore *Sun* he was assigned to write a column that would be readable and irresponsible. According to William Manchester, in pursuit of these goals Mencken ". . . opposed everything respectable, mocked everything sacred, inveighed against everything popular opinion supported. . . . He attacked democracy, Christian Science, osteopathy, the direct primary, the single tax, and every civic improvement boosted by the city fathers. . . . On the lonesome occasion when he did support a popular movement—female suffrage—he did so on the ground that it would quickly reduce democracy to an absurdity."

In espousing the German cause in World War I, Mencken went too far. His column was suspended, and he himself became temporarily an outcast, but he used his enforced leisure to compile *The American Language*, a volume of written and spoken Americanisms. Published after the war, it was an astonishing success. When Mencken joined with the New York drama critic George Jean Nathan and publisher Alfred Knopf to launch a new monthly, *The American Mercury*, it immediately became one of the most widely read of all the highbrow journals.

Mencken's diatribes appeared regularly in his magazine. Of the farmer he wrote, "No more grasping, selfish and dishonest mammal, indeed, is known to students of the anthropoidea"; of democracy, that it was "grounded upon so childish a complex of fallacies that they must be protected by a rigid system of taboos, else even half-wits would argue it to pieces." In an essay "On Being an American," he unlimbered his verbal artillery and asserted that "it is my . . . conviction that the American people, taking one with another, constitute the most timorous, sniveling, poltroonish, ignominious mob of serfs and goosesteppers ever gathered under one flag in Christendom since the end of the Middle Ages, and that they grow more timorous, more sniveling, more poltroonish, more ignominious every day."

To a reader who asked that the *Mercury* present some "constructive points of view," Mencken shot back: "If any such points of view ever get into it, it will only be over my mutilated and pathetic corpse. The uplift has damned nigh ruined the country. What we need is more sin."

Read, reread and widely quoted, such Menckeniana were taken to heart by Americans with intellectual pretensions. On college campuses and in literary salons, Mencken was looked upon as a new prophet. Within a very few years, however, his worshipers would realize that what he preached was a Nietzschean philosophy not unlike that of the Nazis.

The lugubrious novels of Theodore Dreiser (above) had contradictory themes: protests against injustice and demonstrations that man was a helpless victim of environment. "Marching alone, usually unappreciated, often hated," Dreiser "cleared the trail . . . to honesty and boldness and passion of life."

At the time, some of the younger generation were turning away from what was going on and pursuing a life of pure pleasure. Edna St. Vincent Millay's lines echoed this feeling: "My candle burns at both ends; / It will not last the night; / But ah, my foes, and oh, my friends— / It gives a lovely light!"

Another apostle of hedonism, F. Scott Fitzgerald, published his first novel, *This Side of Paradise*, shortly before *Main Street* appeared. In it Fitzgerald glorified a gay, irresponsible, tomorrow-we-die life that had an immediate appeal to young people who, like its central character, felt they had "grown up to find all Gods dead, all wars fought, all faiths in man shaken."

Fitzgerald was not only an exponent of a philosophy but an example. Born in St. Paul, Minnesota, in 1896, he had grown up as a rich boy in a family without money. His father, a salesman, was a failure in business, but his mother's parents had money, and the Fitzgeralds sponged off them. Scott's upbringing in borrowed luxury was followed by two years at prep school, graduation from Princeton and, during the war, commissioned service in the army. (His platoon commander at officer training school was Captain Dwight D. Eisenhower.) When he was 23, Fitzgerald's first novel appeared and made him famous. Immediately afterward he married a beautiful and vivacious Alabama belle. Fitzgerald, strikingly handsome, and his bride Zelda were the very picture of youth and beauty and *joie de vivre*.

Part of the young couple's allure lay in the fact that they were courting tragedy, hastening the day when their candles sputtered out. In two of Fitzgerald's great subsequent novels, *The Beautiful and the Damned* and *The Great Gatsby*, the sense of impending doom grew stronger. His and Zelda's antics gradually became less funny, more frantic. Fitzgerald became an alcoholic. And as he deteriorated, so did Zelda. She became insane and had to be confined in a mental hospital. By the 1930s Fitzgerald, eking out a living around the movie lots in Hollywood, was a piteous figure. But in his person and in his work he had been the beacon of "flaming youth." He had given the Jazz Age its name and, in a sense, he was the Jazz Age.

As the discontents of rural America had come together in a courtroom in Dayton, Tennessee, so those of the Lewises and Menckens conjoined in a courtroom in Dedham, Massachusetts.

On May 5, 1920, Nicola Sacco and Bartolomeo Vanzetti had been arrested

From his incredibly luckless personal life, Eugene O'Neill drew many memorable characters who travel "through a haunted wood of pathos, futility, self-pity and frustration." He is, by common consent, America's greatest playwright; he won four Pulitzer Prizes and the Nobel Prize for Literature.

and charged with participation in a payroll robbery in which two men had been killed. Both men were immigrants from Italy; neither spoke English well; both were anarchists; both had briefly fled America during the war to escape being drafted. When picked up on a Brockton, Massachusetts, street-car, both were armed, their pistols being of the same caliber as those used in the robbery. They were tentatively identified as two of the gunmen and bound over for trial.

Their judge was Webster Thayer, a short, vain, birdlike man who the previous month had tongue-lashed a jury because it had failed to convict a suspected Communist. Though he kept his conduct of the Sacco-Vanzetti trial free from reversible errors, he favored the prosecution wherever he could.

IN his own way the chief defense lawyer also helped the prosecution. A veteran of legal battles for I.W.W. members and strikers, Fred Moore seemed more interested in dramatizing the evidence of class struggle he found in the situation than in freeing his clients. He assumed that Sacco and Vanzetti were not likely to get justice in a courtroom, so he gave more effort to focusing national attention on the trial than to making legal points. Discrepancies in identification were not pursued with vigor, nor were sufficient questions asked about the most damning testimony, a prosecution expert's ambiguous assertion that markings on one of the lethal bullets were "consistent with being fired by [Sacco's] pistol." But by the time the pleadings were in, the district attorney and judge had between them erased all doubts. The jury found the defendants guilty of murder in the first degree.

Moore's publicity efforts had aroused interest in the case. Anarchists and Communists agitated in behalf of the pair. Sensing its opportunity, the Communist International instructed national units to take up the cause. Throughout Europe and Latin America there were demonstrations. Many Italian-Americans, convinced that the men had been victims of prejudice, rallied to them. Meanwhile a number of American liberals joined the rolls of those convinced that an injustice had been done.

Contributions trickled in to pay the costs of appeal. New lawyers were retained and motions were made for another trial on the basis of additional evidence. Though the motions were denied, their argument won time for the condemned men. In 1927 the last legal resort was exhausted. Then the men's lives were in the hands of Governor Alvan Fuller, who could pardon the men or commute their sentences to life imprisonment.

By then the case had assumed awesome proportions with the publication of an article entitled "The Case of Sacco and Vanzetti," by Professor Felix Frankfurter of the Harvard Law School. In simple, compelling terms, Frankfurter argued that the two men were innocent, that they had been victims of the Red scare, and that their appeals had been rejected because conservative judges and public officials refused to concede that the Anglo-American system of justice could make an error.

All over the country, conservatives reacted to Frankfurter's accusation. Pointing out the years that had elapsed since the conviction, they declared that Sacco and Vanzetti had had all the due process men could ask. Former President Taft, now Chief Justice of the United States, characterized the arguments of Frankfurter and other like-minded men as "vicious propaganda." Those momentarily troubled were quieted when Governor Fuller appointed a

Pulitzer Prize-winning poet Edna St. Vincent Millay joined a Boston picket line in 1927 to protest the execution of Sacco and Vanzetti. A large portion of Miss Millay's later poetry was concerned with political questions; however, she was recognized as an outstanding poet chiefly for her earlier writings—love lyrics of extraordinary beauty and understated emotion.

blue-ribbon committee, headed by President Lowell of Harvard, to review the evidence. The committee agreed that Sacco and Vanzetti were "guilty beyond a reasonable doubt." The men died in the electric chair on August 23, 1927.

For most who thought of themselves as intellectuals, there was more than reasonable doubt. Whether this conviction was justified, no one knows. That the trial was not entirely fair seems now beyond doubt, but that the evidence of guilt was stronger than Frankfurter admitted seems equally clear. For intellectuals of the time, however, belief in the innocence of both Sacco and Vanzetti was an article of faith.

To those who followed Lewis or Mencken, the findings of the court and the committee were proof positive of pomposity, narrow-mindedness and arrogance. Mencken wrote that the men were executed solely because they were radicals and foreigners. The Babbitts believed, he sneered, "that Sacco and Vanzetti, being wops, got what was coming to them."

"The Great Gatsby" by F. Scott Fitzgerald (above) received much critical acclaim, but the author's career was blighted by alcoholism. Shortly before his death at 44, he wrote, "When you once get to the point where you don't care whether you live or die—as I did—it's hard to come back to life. . . . It's hard to believe in yourself again —you have slain part of yourself."

The sheer emotional appeal in some of Sacco's and Vanzetti's embittered eloquence gained them many sympathizers. Vanzetti was quoted as saying: "If it had not been for these thing, I might have live out my life talking at street corners to scorning men. I might have die, unmarked, unknown, a failure. Now we are not a failure. This is our career and our triumph. Never in our full life could we hope to do such work for tolerance, for justice, for man's understanding of man, as now we do by an accident."

To those of the flaming-youth generation who were weary of the pursuit of pleasure and of art for art's sake, the Sacco-Vanzetti case offered a new cause that was worth fighting for. John Dos Passos poured out his own feeling into his trilogy *U.S.A.:* "all right you have won you will kill the brave men our friends tonight . . . America our nation has been beaten by strangers who have turned our language inside out who have taken the clean words our fathers spoke and made them slimy and foul . . . all right we are two nations."

When the Depression struck, the Marxian concept of class war—of two nations—was to gain still more appeal. But it was in 1927 that the turn to the far left began. "Don't you see the glory of this case?" asked a character in one of Upton Sinclair's novels, "It kills off the liberals." The unspoken corollary was, of course, that the liberals could now turn only to Communism. As it happened, this was not so and many liberals remained staunchly opposed to totalitarianism even while, almost to a man, they marched or wrote in behalf of Sacco and Vanzetti. But it was as if, all right, there were two nations.

ON the surface, the 1920s were joyous years—the years of the Sunday drive and the big football weekend, the raccoon coat, the speakeasy, Rudolph Valentino and Clara Bow, Dempsey and Tunney, Babe Ruth and Lindbergh —when, as Fitzgerald wrote, "The parties were bigger . . . the pace was faster . . . the shows were broader, the buildings were higher, the morals were looser and the liquor was cheaper."

But this was only one surface. The '20s were also a time when tens of millions of Americans—colored people, rural folk and intellectuals—felt profoundly alienated from the society in which they lived. Looking back on the decade, the nation seemed close to falling apart—not sharply and violently and painfully as in 1861, but fissuring and crumbling like some of the great empires of ancient times. Then tragedy struck and, paradoxically, made the nation one again.

THE KILLERS, Nathan Leopold Jr. *(left)* and Richard Loeb *(right)*, are shown with their lawyer Clarence Darrow during their arraignment in Chicago in 1924. Darrow remarked about the case, "I never saw so much enthusiasm for the death penalty."

A quartet of courtroom classics

IN the '20s technical improvements in radio and press wire services and the syndication of press material made it easy for everyone to enjoy, almost simultaneously, "any good show that came along." The 55 leading newspaper chains controlled more than 230 daily papers with a combined circulation of 13 million. Now the popular press could reduce public events to a series of crowd-pleasing spectacles on a national scale. Thus, although three of the four famous cases described here were of lasting significance, each was treated more as a vaudeville act than a courtroom trial.

The Leopold-Loeb case, in which a pair of psychotic adolescents conducted a gruesome experiment in calculated murder, provided millions of newspaper readers with a vicarious participation in violence. Yet their trial provided the platform from which Clarence Darrow convincingly argued against capital punishment and saved his guilty clients from execution.

In the Scopes case in 1925 a Tennessee high school teacher *(right)* tested the state's anti-evolution law; the trial became the battleground on which rural Fundamentalism lost yet another struggle against the encroachments of an urban secularism. The lurid Hall-Mills case, an unsolved murder of a married clergyman and his mistress, titillated tabloid readers. Nicola Sacco and Bartolomeo Vanzetti were two immigrant anarchists executed for a robbery-murder some six years after they had been convicted of the crime, in an atmosphere of hysterical antiradicalism. During that time their dignified insistence on innocence enlisted the sympathy of people around the world, and for years thereafter, the case was the *cause célèbre* of the American left-wing movement.

THE TEACHER, John Thomas Scopes, who read to his class from a textbook that accepted the theory of evolution, revisits the Dayton courtroom 24 years after his trial.

"Their yells and bawlings fill the air with orthodoxy"

ACCORDING to H. L. Mencken the Scopes trial transformed the sleepy town of Dayton, Tennessee, into the site of "a religious orgy." From the neighboring hill country a steady stream of Bible-carrying farmers and their families flowed into Dayton in old Model Ts and mule-drawn wagons to hear their faith defended against the skepticism of science and "foreigners." Revivalists, weighted down with signs that cautioned the faithful to "come clean" for "Paradise Street is at hand," strode the sweltering streets. Prayer meetings were almost always in session. The hungry gobbled up hot dogs and gulped soft drinks while more than a hundred newspapermen and cameramen watched, scoffed and reported the scene as if it were a circus. After the last bitter exchange between William Jennings Bryan, a champion of the old-fashioned American past, and Clarence Darrow, the liberal defender of the underdog, it became clear that Fundamentalism had lost its battle to test "every fact in science by a religious dictum."

An unexpected confrontation takes place as

The jurors who found Scopes guilty of teaching the Darwinian doctrine are shown seated outside the courtroom during a midday recess.

Darrow and Bryan match wits. The defense called the Great Commoner to testify as a Bible expert, and Darrow slashed at him most of the day.

DARROW LECTURES the jury, gesticulating dramatically during an indoor session. He asked the court to find his client guilty so that the case could be appealed to a higher court. It did, and the State Supreme Court later dismissed the verdict on a technicality.

BRYAN LISTENS. Darrow sneered at Bryan's "fool religion," and was denounced for slurring the Bible.

RECONSTRUCTING THE SCENE, an imaginative painting depicts the two victims and *(from left)* Willie Stevens, Mrs. Hall's dim-witted brother; Ralph Gorsline, a vestryman at the church who had been accused of spying on the lovers; Mrs. Hall's other brother; Mrs. Hall herself; and the "pig woman." The couple was discovered shot to death in a New Jersey

Mr. Hall is flanked by Mrs. Eleanor Mills (left), a choir singer in his church, and Mrs. Hall.

A dying woman's tale of murder most foul

THE sensational trial of Mrs. Frances Hall, her two brothers and a cousin for the murder of the Reverend Edward Hall and his mistress reached its dramatic climax with the appearance of the state's star witness, Jane Easton, alias Jane Gibson, who achieved nationwide fame as the "pig woman" because that was the stock she raised. Stricken with cancer, she testified *(below)* that on the night of the murder, while searching for thieves in her cornfield, she heard voices in nearby De Russey's Lane, saw fighting, a light flash, "something glitter," and heard a gun firing. She ran off. But later, returning to look for a lost moccasin, she recognized Mrs. Hall, "bending down and facing something and crying." Throughout the proceedings the pig woman's mother kept muttering that her daughter was "a liar." This, plus some queer incidents in Mrs. Gibson's past and the questionable testimony of many other witnesses, led the jury to find the defendants not guilty.

The "pig woman" testifies from a bed. Reporters filed some 11 million words on the trial.

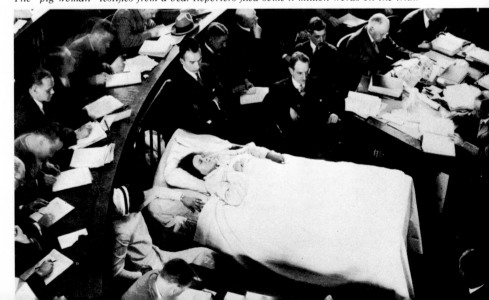

wood, their faces covered. Love letters were scattered over them and Mr. Hall's calling card propped up against his foot.

PROTESTORS in New York demand the unconditional freedom of Sacco and Vanzetti. A force of 1,500 police, armed with tear gas and machine guns, kept order among the 15,000 demonstrators. Most of the sympathizers belonged to minority groups.

A montage by Ben Shahn shows (from left to right) a protest demonstration; Sacco (right) and Vanzetti with Governor Fuller in the background

For the anarchists: execution at home, martyrdom abroad

ALTHOUGH people are still divided about the guilt or innocence of Sacco and Vanzetti, there is now little doubt that the two men were denied the fair trial guaranteed by the Bill of Rights. During their six years of imprisonment, American opinion ranged from enthusiastic approval of the verdict of guilty, to bored indifference, to sympathetic outrage. The Communists busily stirred up international protests on the grounds that the condemned men were working-class martyrs doomed by reactionaries who controlled an unjust legal system. Many non-Communist liberals and leftists joined in supporting Communist-sponsored demonstrations. Overseas, when the men were executed in 1927, roaming bands of marchers destroyed thousands of dollars' worth of American property from London to Moscow.

MANACLED, Vanzetti and Sacco are seen in 1926, after five years in prison. On the day after their execution, the French Communist newspaper *L'Humanité* ran the headline, "Assassinés!"

and the Lowell committee at the anarchists' coffins. These men reviewed the evidence and satisfied Fuller that the pair had had "a fair trial."

6. THE BUBBLE BURSTS

EARLY in the 1920s Florida seemed to be the new El Dorado, where men could strike it rich. In those flush times it was easy for men to convince themselves that a prospering people would leave the cold North to settle in the comfort of sunnier climes. To some extent this actually happened, and as the population of Florida began to grow, land values leaped upward. Promoters took a hand, often hawking unusable jungle or swampland as an investment bound to double, triple or quadruple in value. Prices zoomed until building lots were going for as much as $75,000. Then early in 1926 the real-estate market began to peak out. In the same year two successive hurricanes ravaged the state and inspired second thoughts about the idyllic nature of Florida's climate. In almost no time the bubble burst and prices plummeted.

Few seemed to learn much from this experience, however, and the stock market boom that began a year later made the Florida land rush look tame. Up to that time prices of common and preferred stocks had borne a justifiable relationship to industrial activity. Average prices for common stocks in 1926 were 62 per cent above 1920, an increase that reflected the growth of the automobile, public utilities and entertainment industries, and the consequent increase in construction, oil refining and manufacture of rubber.

The situation was somewhat different with bonds, especially those of foreign governments. Investment houses eager for commissions were paying little attention to long-term prospects for repayment—loans to Peru totaling

A ONE-TERM PRESIDENT, Herbert Hoover is remembered as a political casualty of the Depression. Elected in 1928 by the biggest vote to that date, he was swamped in 1932.

"The Green Pastures," a fanciful interpretation of Negro Bible lore, starred Richard Harrison (above) as "de Lawd." In spite of the Depression, the show ran 18 months, toured 39 states and Canada, and grossed three million dollars before returning to New York for another run. When it first opened in 1930, "Variety" had called it "dreadfully lacking in box-office ability."

$90 million, for example, were judged a "moral and political risk" by the promoter's own analysts. But the major purchasers of bonds were banks seeking higher interest on surplus funds.

Then in 1928 speculation by individuals soared. One of the bankers who helped to bring it on was Charles E. Mitchell, since 1921 president of the National City Bank of New York. Before that time he had headed the National City Company, his bank's investment affiliate, and had preached the gospel of high-pressure selling. Early in his career he would take salesmen to an office window, point out the throngs in the street below and say, "Look down there. There are six million people with average incomes that aggregate thousands of millions of dollars. They are just waiting for someone to come and tell them what to do with their savings."

The older financial elite typified by the Morgan partners may have scorned these tactics at first, but Mitchell's credo had become the watchword in Wall Street by the middle '20s. Contests spurred salesmen's efforts—Mitchell, for example, offered $25,000 in prizes for the top producers. Letters from home offices demanded aggressiveness, high-pressure tactics and, above all, results.

Bankers like Mitchell, victims of acute overoptimism, truly believed in their wares. John J. Raskob, a director of General Motors, chairman of the Democratic National Committee and a promoter of the Empire State Building, wrote in the *Ladies' Home Journal*: "Suppose a man . . . begins a regular savings of $15 a month. . . . If he invests in good common stocks, and allows the dividends and rights to accumulate, he will, at the end of twenty years, have at least $80,000 and an income from investments of around $400 a month. . . . I am firm in my belief that anyone not only can be rich, but ought to be rich."

THERE are no accurate figures on how many people actually took part in the stock-buying spree of 1928-1929. Member firms of the New York Stock Exchange had 1,371,920 accounts in their books. It seems probable that the total number of accounts in brokerage houses throughout the country did not exceed 1,550,000. Of these it is estimated that 950,000 were cash accounts, presumably nonspeculative, in which customers paid in full for each share they bought. There were about 600,000 margin, presumably speculative, accounts, in which a customer put up only part of the purchase money, securing a loan from his broker to cover the rest. The broker received interest on his loan—he had in turn borrowed the money from a bank, using the securities purchased by margin customers as collateral for his loan. In this way the speculative cycle was established and kept running. The essential ingredient needed to keep the system going was a continuing rise in stock prices.

Some price rises were due entirely to manipulative bidding among banking houses, some resulted from public eagerness to take part in the boom. But in the light of the relatively small numbers of individuals who were speculating, it may be that the inflation in security values was brought on as much through the idiocy of suckers at the very top of the financial community as through avidity of suckers from the hinterland. In any case, the market went upward.

The number of shares traded on the New York Exchange leaped from 449 million in 1926 to 576 million in 1927 to 920 million in 1928, and 1,124,000,000 in 1929. The average of common-stock prices in the Standard Statistics Index, which had stood at 96.9 in June 1926, was at 216.1 in 1929—up 123 per cent in 39 months. During 1928 Wright Aeronautics went from 69 to 289, Du Pont from 310 to 525, Montgomery Ward from 117 to 440 and Radio Corporation of America, pre-eminently the symbol of the big bull market, from 85 to 420.

Small-scale speculators were entering the market in larger numbers. On one of his trips to New York in the late '20s, F. Scott Fitzgerald found that his favorite barber had retired, having made $500,000 in the stock market. Trust executors and small-town bankers shifted funds out of business loans and government bonds into stocks. The moguls of Wall Street assured them that the stocks could only go up.

I N the years since the crash of 1929, economists have been searching for definitive answers to the questions of whether or not the cataclysmic collapse was foreseeable and what were the significant factors that made this the most serious and prolonged financial crisis in American history. On the first point, there is conflicting evidence. One important economic indicator, the level of residential construction, had been falling for several years before 1929, a significant warning that in a time when housing was needed, many could not afford to buy. Industrial production, on the other hand, remained encouragingly high until June of that year, when a decline began.

However, there were deeper indications of a lack of soundness in the economy that—had they been taken into account—portended a day of reckoning. Harvard economist J. K. Galbraith summarized these in *The Great Crash:*

1) Maldistribution of income. Five per cent of the population received in 1929 about one third of all personal income. Any curtailment in spending or investment by these very rich people would produce violent financial reactions.

2) The shaky corporate organization. Proliferation of dubiously financed holding companies and investment trusts multiplied any distress at the operating level by the number of tiers of paper superstructure erected by the financial wizards of the time.

3) A weak banking system made up of large numbers of independent units. Failure of one led to runs on others.

4) The international balance of trade. During World War I, America had become a creditor rather than a debtor nation; foreign countries owed the United States considerable sums. The deficit might have been made up by increased exports to the U.S., but high American tariffs made this almost impossible. The alternatives were to ship gold or secure loans. Loans were floated in Wall Street. But tariffs went still higher, loans were defaulted and American investors were badly hurt. The Depression fed on these disasters.

5) The straitjacket of classical economic theory. This made it sinful for the government to take any affirmative action that might have ameliorated the worst effects of the crash.

To a certain extent the preceding analysis reflects the wisdom of hindsight. It should be said that during the halcyon times before the crash, there had been occasional warnings—from President Hoover, the Federal Reserve Bank and some economists—that the situation might be getting out of hand. However only a lonely, gloomy few, like banker Paul M. Warburg, stock market analyst Roger Babson and certain financial writers, saw anything really frightening in the state of the nation.

October 24, 1929, a day that would be known afterward as Black Thursday, opened ominously on the New York Stock Exchange. There had been considerable selling for several days, and prices had tumbled badly. Calls for more

The "emancipated woman" of the '20s was a potential gold mine for the tobacco companies. At times their advertising strategy was a bit bashful—the young lady seen above is merely offering a smoke to her escort. But ads were also making direct appeals to the ladies: Lucky Strike (below) boldly claimed that its cigarettes could help them to control their weight.

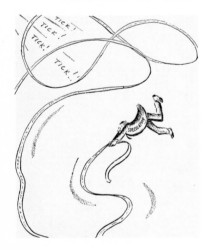

The term "bear market," legend says, originated when one speculator sold a bearskin before catching the bear. The bear which ravaged Wall Street in 1929 (above) left ruin in its wake. Investors struggled to hang on (below), but many ended up broke. Clerks in New York hotels, the joke went, began asking guests if they wanted a room for sleeping—or for jumping.

margin had gone out. This meant that the value of particular securities had sunk to a point where they no longer offered sufficient collateral for loans that had been made to purchase them. Unless more cash were put up, the security would be sold by the broker to protect his loan.

On Thursday brokers were selling out shares owned by speculators who had been unable to raise more cash. The number of such accounts, it developed, ran into the thousands. Most brokers wanted to sell, few to buy. Prices sagged. As the day went on, more margin accounts had to be liquidated, and traders who owned shares outright became uneasy. "Fear struck the big speculators and little ones, big investors and little ones . . ." said the New York *Times*, "thousands of them threw their holdings into the whirling Stock Exchange pit for what they would bring." On the big board, where a five-million-share day was considered quite high, 12,894,650 shares changed hands. Tickers fell hours behind.

In the 1907 crash the elder J. P. Morgan had marshaled the financial community, poured in money to buttress the prices of strategic stocks and staved off collapse. At noon on October 24, 1929, Morgan's successors hurriedly summoned a meeting of the banking titans. Mitchell of the National City, Albert H. Wiggin of the Chase National, George F. Baker of the First National, William C. Potter of the Guaranty Trust and Seward Prosser of the Bankers Trust met with Thomas W. Lamont of the Morgan house. Each banker agreed to put up a large sum to support the market. Soon afterward Richard Whitney, vice president of the Stock Exchange and brother of a Morgan partner, placed large buying orders for 15 or 20 pivotal issues. Prices rallied somewhat, and when the transactions were finally totaled a number of issues proved to have recovered ground.

Financiers issued confident statements. Lamont said there had merely been "a little distress selling" due to a "technical condition of the market." Merrill Lynch and Company advised its customers to "take advantage of this break to buy good securities." Some of the favorite speculative stocks had nevertheless wound up 25 to 30 points below their opening prices, and despite all reassurances, margin traders, investors and brokers felt the pinch of fear.

Friday and Saturday saw heavy trading but without sharp price declines. Brokers then spent the weekend going over accounts and asking customers to put up more margin. When the exchanges reopened on Monday, prices went down again. On Tuesday, October 29, the bottom dropped out.

ON that disastrous day 16,410,030 shares were traded at the Stock Exchange. Practically every issue fell: Allied Chemical was down 35, American Can down 16, American Foreign Power down 22½, American Telephone and Telegraph down 28, and so on through the alphabet. The New York *Times* estimated that at least eight billion dollars in paper values had vanished on the New York Stock Exchange.

Financiers still spoke soothingly of the coming upswing. Actually the 40 governors of the New York Exchange had met secretly on Tuesday. Only after long deliberation did they decide to keep the exchange open. The bankers' pool of Black Thursday was no longer in evidence. Indeed, men like Mitchell and Wiggin, who had juggled bank stocks for their own speculations, could think of nothing but saving themselves. The plight of banks and corporations that had been pleased to lend their funds to brokers (who had promptly used the money to finance their margin customers) was desperate. More than one institution claiming assets in the hundreds of millions faced ruin.

Though no single day that followed was quite as bad as Black Thursday and Terrifying Tuesday, prices fell steadily. By mid-November the total loss on paper, for the New York Stock Exchange alone, was $30 billion.

DEPRESSION, soon to be known as the Great Depression, settled in slowly. In 1930 the gross national product, or market value of total goods and services of the national economy, dropped to $91 billion from the $104 billion of 1929. In 1931 the total figure was down to $76 billion and in 1932 it hit $58.5 billion. Industrial production followed along. With the figures for 1923 to 1925 as 100, the industrial-production index went from 119 in 1929 to 96 in 1930 to 81 in 1931, and 64 in 1932. Bank failures meanwhile rose from 642 in 1929 to 1,345 the next year and 2,298 in 1931. Unemployment climbed from 1,550,000 in 1929 to a staggering estimate of 12,060,000 by 1932. (That was actually one of the lower estimates. Others ran as high as 16 million.)

As the Depression intensified, it seemed as though everybody had a story about a former rich man who had to file papers in bankruptcy or live on peanuts from a vending machine. In fact, there were relatively few of these instances. The story also spread that many speculators jumped from their office windows; few did so.

Much more distressed were people whose prosperity had consisted only of a car, a house and some household goods, all owned on credit. While most employers were slow to fire employees, they did cut back working hours. Eventually they reduced wages, and as the Depression went into a second and then a third year, laid off workers or closed up whole departments. Meanwhile salesmen's commissions dwindled, the fees of professional men went unpaid, and the salaries for clergymen, schoolteachers and civil servants went down. In Chicago 1,000 public-school teachers had been fired by 1933, those still working took a slice in salary—and the salary itself was paid in promissory notes of the city that could be exchanged for cash only at a discount.

The industrial workers and the farmers were the first and the hardest hit. But by 1932 the great divide was no longer between white-collar and factory workers; now it was simply between those who had jobs of any kind and those who did not. Some of the unemployed took to the streets, shining shoes, peddling newspapers or selling apples. Others, after discovering that no jobs were to be had, stayed at home—at least as long as they had homes. Many were in what might be called "unemployment shock," a condition bringing with it listlessness, loss of appetite, loss of concern with personal cleanliness and other symptoms of retreat from reality.

Some who lost their homes drifted into shantytowns that mushroomed around city dumps. There they improvised shelters of rusted auto bodies, makeshift tents or hovels built of cardboard and scrap tin. These communities—found all over the country—came to be known as Hoovervilles. Some people just drifted, becoming hoboes who hitchhiked, hopped freights and begged or stole to stay alive.

No part of the country escaped the ravages of the Depression. Farmers, in difficulty before the crash, were evicted by the tens of thousands. In 1932 Oscar Ameringer, an editor, testified before a House committee on labor about a three-month tour that covered some 20 states: "In the State of Washington

Richard Whitney, the young and confident "White Knight of Wall Street," was elected president of the New York Stock Exchange in 1930. Eight years later the public was shocked when he was sent to prison for some highly irregular stock transactions. Inmates were awed by the important new convict, who went to work as a prison office clerk—at 15 cents a day.

I was told that the forest fires raging in that region all summer and fall were caused by unemployed timber workers and bankrupt farmers in an endeavor to earn a few honest dollars as fire fighters. The last thing I saw on the night I left Seattle was numbers of women searching for scraps of food in the refuse piles. . . . While Oregon sheep raisers fed mutton to the buzzards I saw men picking for meat scraps in the garbage cans in the cities of New York and Chicago. . . . We have overproduction and underconsumption at the same time and in the same country."

New terms—"Hooverville," "Hoover hog" for a jack rabbit and "Hoover blanket" for the newspaper that covered a man who slept on a park bench— evidenced a growing feeling that the leaders of government, and President Hoover in particular, deserved the blame for the downward plunge of the economy. In retrospect, a fairer appraisal of the President would be that within the limits imposed by circumstances and his convictions, Hoover did work to stem the Depression.

In the early '30s produce prices fell so low that many a farmer destroyed his crops rather than pay to market them. When some farmers in New York could get only a cent a pint for milk, they stopped their shipments. The dairyman above is dumping his milk in the vain hope of forcing prices up.

A FAR abler man than either Harding or Coolidge, Hoover's talents had made him one of the foremost construction engineers in the world. He had retired at 40, several times a millionaire. Subsequently, as head of Belgian relief, the wartime Food Administration and the postwar Commerce Department, he earned a reputation as an energetic and farsighted administrator.

As President he had accomplished significant administrative reforms, including reorganization of the F.B.I. and wide improvements in the federal prison system. He brought order into federal conservation programs, sponsored the Boulder (or Hoover) and Grand Coulee Dams and gave commercial aviation a needed boost by subsidizing airmail. Hoover also tried, though ineffectually, to solve the problem of farm surpluses. After the Depression set in, he had the courage to proclaim a one-year moratorium on payments by European countries of their World War I debts to the United States government.

During the war his heart had gone out to the Belgians; in the postwar famine he was deeply moved by the plight of starving Russians. In 1927, when floods washed through the Mississippi Valley, he was everywhere—mobilizing food, clothing and shelter for the victims. Had Hoover held office in a less troubled time, he might have been accounted one of the better Presidents. But with all his compassion and all his experience, he was incapable either of seeing the Depression as an emergency comparable to a flood or of bringing himself to use the weapons for which the emergency called.

In his inaugural address he had said, "Ours is a land rich in resources . . . blessed with comfort and opportunity. In no nation are the fruits of accomplishment more secure. . . . I have no fear for the future of our country." At the pit of the Depression, he retained his conviction that the American economy was "on a sound and prosperous basis," and he repeatedly proclaimed this belief until the words mocked themselves.

Hoover regarded the downturn as temporary. He refused to believe that large numbers of people were actually starving, and consistently discounted estimates of unemployment. When at last he acknowledged that the slump was a continuing one, he put the blame on Europe—on England's desertion of the gold standard and on overproduction of raw materials by other nations.

When the Depression began, Hoover relied on exhortation. He urged businessmen to be optimistic, buy raw materials while prices were down, maintain the level of employment and wages, and count on sales to rise. To public officials he pointed out the opportunity to build roads, schools and public buildings at less than normal costs; he set an example by accelerating construction of previously planned highways, dams and office buildings.

As the situation got worse, Hoover directed his sermons at the general public. Show faith in the economy, he preached, by buying instead of hoarding. In early fall 1931, he implored people to give to private charitable organizations during a special drive. Sad to relate, this drive—like the campaigns for business confidence and public spending—accomplished almost nothing.

When Congress repeatedly asked that federal funds be used for relief of the needy, Hoover fought back. It was argued that if there were taxation for a federal relief program, people would cease giving to private and community organizations, further injuring the unemployed. When a federal relief bill came up in the Senate a coalition of conservative Republicans and Southern Democrats blocked it. As one critic observed, the result was "to save starving Americans the humiliation of being fed by their government. . . ."

Later on Hoover was to summarize his philosophy of government's place in national welfare: "The humanism of our system demands the protection of the suffering and the unfortunate. It places prime responsibility upon the individual for the welfare of his neighbor, but it insists also that in necessity the local community, the State government, and in the last resort, the National government shall give protection to them." What he envisioned as "protection" no one knows, for in his mind "the last resort" never arrived while he was in office.

Hoover went as far as his convictions and conscience permitted. Finally he had to admit that something more than private action was called for, and he made tentative moves in the direction of government action. With some trepidation, he created a federal bank to prevent foreclosures of home mortgages. Hoover's concern for the protection of the power, independence and privileges of private business made him more enthusiastic about establishing the Reconstruction Finance Corporation, which used federal funds for loans to shore up shaky financial institutions, corporations and railroads. But the President never envisioned the RFC as more than a temporary agency having limited functions. When Congress got out of hand in 1932 and gave the RFC $300 million for loans to states, for relief programs, Hoover signed the act only after certain sections were rewritten.

Renominated by his party, he campaigned in 1932 for a second term, saying: "It is not the function of the government to relieve individuals of their responsibilities to their neighbors, or to relieve private institutions of their responsibilities to the public. . . ."

To oppose Hoover, the Democrats nominated a fifth cousin of Theodore Roosevelt, Franklin D. Roosevelt of New York. As a young man, Roosevelt won a surprising victory as the Democratic candidate for the state senate in the usually Republican district around Hyde Park. Roosevelt's work for Wilson in 1912 had been rewarded by appointment as Assistant Secretary of the Navy. In 1920 Roosevelt was his party's vice presidential candidate. But in 1921, while vacationing at Campobello Island off New Brunswick, he had been stricken with poliomyelitis. His legs were permanently paralyzed, and most politicians thought his career was finished. He did not. From his

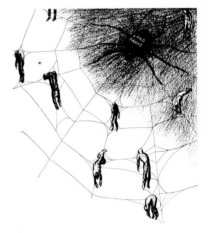

Under federal sponsorship, land banks were formed in 1916 to aid agriculture. But in making easy farm loans, these banks trapped farmers in a web of mortgages (above). Broke when the Depression struck, many farmers faced what one lawmaker bitterly called "the desirable foreclosure process."

The sound of the auctioneer's hammer sent thousands of dispossessed families from their farms in helpless anger (above). Sometimes their tempers snapped. In Iowa farmers threatened to lynch an agent of a New York firm for his low bid. The frantic buyer wired for $3,000 more, adding, "My neck at risk."

sickbed he continued a correspondence with party leaders the state and nation over. In 1924, burdened by heavy leg braces, he dragged himself to the rostrum in Madison Square Garden to nominate Governor Alfred E. Smith, felicitously calling him "the Happy Warrior." In 1928 Roosevelt bucked the strong Republican tide to win election as Governor of New York.

On the state level Roosevelt faced the problems created by the Depression and in coping with them showed not only courage and vigor but a wholly undogmatic willingness to experiment. He talked of much larger spending for public works and of unemployment insurance. He was the first governor to set up a state-wide relief agency that went beyond doling out food and clothing and attempted to create jobs for the destitute. "To . . . unfortunate citizens," he said, "aid must be extended by the government—not as a matter of charity but as a matter of social duty."

T HE Democratic delegates who gathered at Chicago in 1932 did not nominate Roosevelt solely because he had been adventurous. Indeed, those who leaned toward radical solutions for the Depression were dubious of his commitment to Federal intervention. They pointed to the fact that while he seemed to be an advocate of public works and relief and of doing something for "the forgotten man at the bottom of the economic pyramid," he also favored governmental economy and had condemned Hoover for his unbalanced budgets. Political commentator Walter Lippmann dismissed him as "a pleasant man who, without any important qualifications for the office, would very much like to be President." For conservative delegates, Roosevelt's principal competitors for the nomination—Al Smith, Governor Albert Ritchie of Maryland, Speaker of the House John Nance Garner of Texas and ex-Secretary of War Newton D. Baker of Ohio—had far more convincing qualifications. But Roosevelt won the nomination partly because of his name, his charm and the mixture of gaiety, confidence and courage that he radiated. These qualifications, plus, some say, a deal made with Garner's chief backer, William Randolph Hearst, gave Roosevelt the accolade on the fourth ballot.

His acceptance speech promised "a new deal for the American people." During the campaign the crowds greeting Hoover were apathetic, sometimes hostile, while those greeting Roosevelt were large and responsive. Garner, the vice presidential nominee, said that all Roosevelt had to do to win was live until election day. Roosevelt remained bland and equivocal, giving only faint glimmerings of what his "new deal" might be.

Around him, however, were already gathered the men and women who would give that phrase an unforgettable substance. From the academic world came the "brain trust" recruited by Raymond Moley, a professor at Columbia University. Old progressives Harold Ickes and Donald Richberg from Chicago; ex-Republican Henry Wallace from Iowa; and Hugh Johnson, an ex-Army general who dreamed of whipping big business into line as Baruch had done during World War I—all were there. Baruch himself was there, and so was Joseph P. Kennedy, the Boston millionaire who had sold his shares before the crash and knew every trick in the financial game.

In the middle of this turmoil was the candidate himself, "all grin and gusto" on the outside, as Arthur Schlesinger Jr. has written, but "terribly hard inside . . . a man without illusions, clearheaded and compassionate, who had been close enough to death to understand the frailty of human striving,

In Washington the veterans in the 1932 "Bonus March" were stunned to find that men wearing their old uniform would act against them. As cavalry rode down a group of ex-soldiers, a spectator cried, "The American flag means nothing to me after this." One veteran had said before he left for the capital: "I might as well starve there as here." He was shot dead by police.

but who remained loyal enough to life to do his best in the sight of God."

In November the voters responded much as predicted. Roosevelt got 22,809,638 votes to Hoover's 15,758,901. The 20th Amendment to the Constitution, moving inauguration day to January, had not yet taken effect, so that it was to be March 1933 before the energies and capacities of the new Administration would be put on trial.

In the summer of 1932 the "Bonus Expeditionary Force," made up of 20,000 ragged veterans of World War I, had arrived in Washington to petition Congress for prepayment of a bonus for wartime service, not due until 1945. Camping in abandoned buildings and a giant Hooverville on the Anacostia Flats, the veterans stirred more and more alarm among government officials. Congress turned down the petition. Then some of the veterans had a brush with the police. This was the signal for drastic orders from Secretary of War Patrick J. Hurley, approved by Hoover. The Army chief of staff, General Douglas MacArthur, leading four troops of cavalry, six tanks and a column of infantry, destroyed the encampment and drove the veterans and their wives and children into Maryland. Later MacArthur claimed, despite overwhelming evidence to the contrary, that the veterans, "a mob . . . animated by the essence of revolution," had been about to seize control of the government.

In Philadelphia, New York, Chicago and other cities, Communist-led unemployed conducted hunger marches. In Iowa, ex-Populist Milo Reno organized a farm-holiday movement which threatened to stop all shipments of food to cities unless prices for their products were raised. From one end of the country to the other, people fearfully whispered the word "revolution."

The Bonus Expeditionary Force, hunger marches and farmers' uprisings were phenomena of the summer and early autumn of 1932. As winter approached, the number of demonstrations dropped, perhaps because of cold, perhaps because of hope for the promised "new deal." But it needed brave optimism for anyone to predict a happy future for the republic.

Anyone who lifted his eyes beyond the continental limits could find further cause for pessimism. In September 1931 the Japanese had marched into Manchuria. In the Japanese army, talk mounted of a campaign to conquer China. In Europe Fascist Italy was arming and dictator Benito Mussolini was boasting that his nation would build a new Roman Empire. In Berlin on January 30, 1933, the doddering president of the German republic, former Field Marshal Paul von Hindenburg, named as chancellor the ranting Brownshirt leader, Adolf Hitler. As Franklin Roosevelt's inauguration approached, wherever one looked the future seemed big with trouble.

I N the lifetime of men still vigorous in 1932, a country of farms had become one of factories, a horse-and-buggy era had given way to an age of automobiles and airplanes. The extremes of wealth and poverty, of power and impotence, had intensified. The national government, which a few years before had been entrusted by a huge vote to a man who took pride in keeping his hands off the economy, was now looked to as the last best hope of rescue from the Depression. In the midst of prosperity, the march of progress had seemed omnipotent. Now there was reason for doubt—for wonder whether there was not some truth in Clemenceau's cynical epigram that the United States was the only nation in history to have gone from barbarism to decadence without the usual interval of civilization.

Four-star General Douglas MacArthur and Major Dwight Eisenhower appear together in 1932, when MacArthur's troops routed the Bonus Army. Eisenhower had little if anything to do with the debacle, but in 1952 when he was running for President, opponents tried to discredit him by circulating the picture under the headline "Gen. Ike Helps Rout Vets."

UNWELCOME in Washington in 1932 is an army of jobless veterans that had marched there in an effort to collect their bonus payments 13 years in advance. On July 28 their shanties were burned and the men dispersed by armed U.S. troops.

Fads, fashions and mass lunacy

THE sound of the '20s was, indeed, a roar—a mixed roar of pleasure at being alive, of astonishment at being free from old taboos, of bewilderment at a new order. To a considerable extent, science was responsible for the look of novelty that was a hallmark of the decade. But in the spirit of the time, few of the technical changes of the '20s represented breakthroughs achieved by pure science; they were rather the bustling application of laboratory findings to meet everyday needs and wants. Refrigerators, washing machines and other household appliances, powered by ever more widely available electricity, meant less work for the housewife. The automobile gave a new sense of freedom. The telegraph, telephone, tabloid, radio and movies brought the outside world right into the middle of Main Street. Even remote villages, formerly placid backwaters of traditional thought and manners, were no longer moated off from the ferment of disturbing ideas new and old—like those of Darwin, who had demonstrated mankind's descent from lower animals, and those of Freud, who had announced that men, more than they realized, were motivated by sex drives. Sex had arrived. Manners and morals took a beating; so did law and order. The 18th Amendment to the Constitution made prohibition the law, but who cared? "Yes, We Have No Bananas" was the song everyone was singing. But there were plenty of bathing beauties, murder trials, mah-jongg, short skirts, crazy dances, sports heroes, real-estate booms, stock market booms—and at the end of a wild decade, a bust.

WELCOME of the '20s, New York style, is personified by Grover Whalen, the city's long-time official greeter, here seen recalling parades for everybody who was anybody.

Survivors of the Bunion Derby—a marathon on which promoter C. C. "Cash and Carry" Pyle lost heavily—ford the Hudson by ferry. Andy

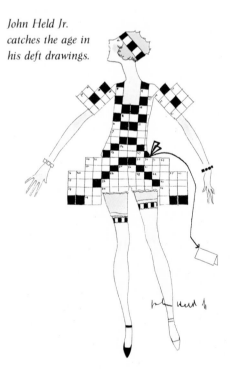

John Held Jr. catches the age in his deft drawings.

THE 3,327TH HOUR of a dance marathon is recorded in Chicago. The couple will be eliminated if her sagging knees touch the floor.

Payne (far left) won the 84-day jog from Los Angeles to New York City.

Avid thumpers of brassy ballyhoo drums

THE '20s spawned fads and contests in endless variety. Each new day saw some new development reported on the front page of the papers. Anyone who could do anything longer or harder or faster than anyone else was a champion, and it didn't matter of what—running, dancing, sitting on flagpoles, swimming, flying, riding a bicycle, walking or driving.

Hungry promoters around the country, noting public reaction to such genuine heroism as Lindbergh's solo flight to Paris, thought up harebrained schemes to make a fast buck. Others pushed fads like mah-jongg that swept the country overnight. These entrepreneurs had learned how to mass-produce sensation almost as well as other Americans produced automobiles, and it is a fine question as to which group showed more ingenuity. Anything, it seemed, would sell if it was nutty enough.

NUTTIEST CRAZE of the '20s, flagpole sitting, sees "Shipwreck" Kelly, his arms outflung, during one of these unbelievable stunts. He set the 23-day 7-hour record.

A golden age of sports when champions were gods

BIG-TIME sport came of age in the '20s. Americans emerged from the war with a certain amount of leisure on their hands. Bookkeepers and milkmen took up golf, once the exclusive province of the rich. Men who had never seen a course bought the latest editions to follow Bobby Jones's progress in the British Amateur Golf Tournament. Others whose education stopped with high school traveled to New Haven to watch the Har-vards play the Yales. In 1921 the Babe hit 59 home runs. Two years later the Yankees moved into their new park, "the house that Ruth built." A nationwide communications system, improved by commercial radio early in the decade, brought sports news into every parlor. In 1925, Red Grange's last year as Illinois' hero, few Americans knew the name of the Postmaster General, but almost anyone could tell you who carried the ball for the Illini.

A great moment of boxing is caught by George Bellows as heavyweight champ Jack Dempsey hurtles out of the ring. He climbed back to knock

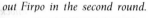

Top schools set the standards for Joe College.

BOBBY JONES rules the golf world. He climaxed his great career in 1930 by winning the "impregnable quadrilateral" —the U.S. and British Open and Amateur championships.

SATURDAY'S HERO is Red Grange. He did well on other days too, with the aid of a $300,000 movie deal.

out Firpo in the second round.

THE BABE, the Bambino, the Sultan of Swat, are some of the many names fans had for George Herman Ruth. He came to the Yankees in 1920 and thrilled the country that year by hitting an unheard-of 54 home runs. He went right on hitting them through the decade, scoring his record 60 in 1927.

WILLIAM TILDEN II sets a new tennis style. Part hero, part ham, he aroused a gallery as did no other court champion of the day.

GERTRUDE EDERLE, first woman to swim the English Channel, prepares for her feat. In 1926 she beat the men's mark by 2 hours 23 minutes.

143

The Pied Piper plays a saxophone.

A country jumping to a jazzy rhythm

A funeral offers a fine excuse for a New Orleans band to cut loose. The noise the musicians made had a life-giving beat that marched right out

An old man who had lived in New Orleans, and who remembered taking part in funeral processions similar to the one shown below, recalled how it was: "On the way out to the cemetery, before they bury the man, the band played most all hymns, like 'Just a Closer Walk with Thee.' But once they left there, then they started to swing. They wouldn't be 25 feet from the graveyard before they hit 'Didn't He Ramble.' . . . Then they'd play 'Sing On' or 'The Saints.' The kids would come a running, wanting to jump. So they'd form that second line beside the band. . . . Finally the band would get to the lodge hall and break up and that was always the end of a perfect death."

From such origins, and from spirituals, old ballads, children's jingles, minstrel music and the ragtime piano of red-light districts, jazz was born. When it came up to Chicago in the early '20s, jazz found a home in the sinister world of gangsters and speakeasies. Soon short-skirted debutantes from New York to San Francisco were wiggling and jiggling to that same tantalizing beat.

of town clear up the Mississippi to Chicago. Then it kept moving until it had spread from ocean to ocean and crossed the Atlantic to Europe.

Sandwiched between a farmerette and a party scene is a painting by Norman Rockwell. He did more than 300 "Post" covers from 1916 on.

Magazines shunning reality, glorifying the ideal

OF the fast-changing pace, the new thoughts, the emphasis on good times, sex and wild living—in short, of all that made the '20s roar—no better record exists than that found in the leading magazines of the era.

Not everyone was doing the Charleston, as the cover of the old *Life* shown here might suggest, but dancing certainly flourished. Under the elegant guidance of Condé Nast, the era's taste-setting publisher, *Vogue* set the fashions for the nation's elite, with a hand from Hearst's *Harper's Bazar*. *The Saturday Evening Post*, accused by its critics of being devoted to "crass materialism," was tremendously popular in an era devoted to the same end. As a careful examination of the names on some of the covers pictured here will reveal, many top-notch writers published stories in such elegant showcases as the *Delineator*, *Harper's Bazar* and even the "crass" *Post*.

Milady's fashions, interlarded with a modicum of serious writing, make up these three publications, highly successful during the '20s.

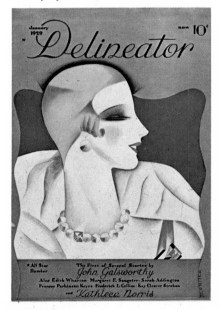

One of John Held Jr.'s flappers is featured on this 1926 issue of "Life." Moribund by 1936, the humor magazine sold its name to Time Inc.

The Roxy's interior presents a gaudy conglomeration of Gothic form, Renaissance detail and Moorish atmosphere. Completed in 1927, the lavish

The movies are suddenly a monster business.

A stately pleasure dome housing a new religion

FOR preposterous grandiosity and unblushing bad taste, nothing produced during the '20s could equal the movie palaces. Hollywood had created a new religion with a dazzling galaxy of gods and goddesses like Rudolph Valentino and Pola Negri. It was not long before a crafty priesthood had erected fabulous temples —the Rivieras, Tivolis and Rialtos—where for a small sum the idolatrous public could be transported to the very gates of paradise. When Samuel L. "Roxy" Rothafel built the largest cinema of its day—the 6,214-seat, $12 million Roxy Theatre that rose in majesty a few blocks from Times Square—it seemed only fitting that he should subtitle his creation "The Cathedral of the Motion Picture." Its ritual dances were performed by a carefully matched corps of 36 young women called Roxyettes, and it had its own army of 125 elegantly uniformed ushers.

THE DEAD "SHEIK," Rudolph Valentino, attracts a host of the curious, who queue up in the rain to see their embalmed idol. Shrewd press agents had turned Valentino's untimely death at 31 into an orgy of grief.

149

TERRIFYING TUESDAY, to James Rosenberg, attorney-artist, seems "like the end of America"; his lithograph conveys the impact of the crash.

October 24, 1929: the day the bull market died

IT did not really happen on a single day. The structure of the stock market had been unsteady for months, as if some great, elemental force were stirring beneath it. But each time a crack had appeared, somehow it had been covered. Then, late in October 1929, there came a day when the cracks kept on opening until the whole crazy structure fell to pieces. It took a dozen years and the eve of war to put the economy back together.

When the big bull market died, billions of dollars worth of paper profits died with it. Little investors, the clerks and grocerymen who had "played the market" with the few dollars they could scrape together each week, saw their dreams smashed. On Wall Street paper fortunes disappeared overnight; a few of the losers chose to commit suicide rather than face the future. In towns across the nation, there were families that dropped from showy affluence into debt. The crash triggered a chain of calamities that blighted almost every level of American society. More than three decades later, the mere mention of the year still evokes memories of disaster.

DAZED SPECTATORS stand transfixed in front of the Stock Exchange on the terrible day when frantic speculators tried in vain to meet the calls for additional margin.

CHRONOLOGY *A timetable of American and world events: 1917-1932*

WORLD EVENTS	EVENTS OF WORLD WAR I	POLITICS	MILITARY and FOREIGN AFFAIRS	ECONOMICS and SCIENCE	THOUGHT and CULTURE
1917 Finland proclaims independence 1917 Moderate revolution in Russia followed by Bolshevist coup 1917 International Red Cross in Geneva wins Nobel Peace Prize 1918 Max Planck of Germany wins Nobel Prize in Physics 1918 Treaty of Brest-Litovsk between Russia and Central Powers 1918 Murder of Russian royal family 1918 Germany deposes Kaiser; declares a republic 1918 Dismemberment of Austro-Hungarian Empire 1918 Formation of Baltic republics	April 6, 1917 U.S. declares war on Germany May 1917 Selective service inaugurated June 1917 Pershing starts fight for integral U.S. Army with its own sector of front June 1917 U.S. troops begin combat training in France March 1918 Germans begin their spring offensive April 1918 Lys defensive shores up British lines May-July 1918 German advance on the Marne stopped at Château-Thierry June-July 1918 Independent U.S. action at Belleau Wood July-Aug. 1918 Second Battle of the Marne—turning point of the war July-Aug. 1918 Allies take offensive on Aisne-Marne line Aug. 1918 British-American Somme offensive Aug. 1918 French-American Oise-Aisne offensive Sept. 1918 Americans capture Saint-Mihiel salient Sept. 1918 General Ludendorff presses German government for armistice Sept.-Nov. 1918 Meuse-Argonne campaign Nov. 11, 1918 Armistice	1917 Formation of Committee on Public Information, headed by George Creel 1917 Espionage Act empowers prosecutions and censorship 1917 18th (prohibition) Amendment submitted to states by Congress 1917 Supreme Court narrowly sustains the 1916 Adamson Act specifying eight-hour day on interstate railroads 1918 Supreme Court upholds constitutionality of 1917 Selective Service Act 1918 1916 Child Labor Act declared unconstitutional 1918 Antiwar socialist leaders imprisoned under Sedition Act 1918 Wilson appeals for a Democratic congressional victory 1918 Republicans control both houses of Congress	1917 Lansing-Ishii Agreement recognizes Japan's special interest in northern China 1917-19 War casualties in U.S. armed forces total 349,000, including 112,000 dead 1917-20 Direct U.S. war expenses total $32.8 billion 1918 Wilson issues the Fourteen Points, a summary of American war aims 1918 Wilson announces he will attend the peace conference	1917 Smith-Hughes Act establishes Federal Board for Vocational Education 1917 Increased income tax helps raise wartime revenue 1917 Herbert Hoover becomes food administrator, Harry Garfield named fuel administrator under Lever Act 1917 Steel production of 45,060,607 long tons almost doubles that of 1914 1917-18 President gives extensive regulatory power over wartime economy to War Industries Board, headed by Bernard Baruch 1917-19 Liberty Bonds totaling $21.5 billion issued 1917-20 Railroads nationalized as wartime measure 1918 Export trade exempted from antitrust legislation 1918 Creation of National War Labor Board 1918 National Research Council permanently established 1918-19 Influenza epidemic kills more than 500,000 in U.S. alone	1917 Inauguration of Pulitzer Prize awards; Herbert Bayard Swope wins one for reporting 1917 First recording of a jazz band 1918 Commonwealth Fund established 1918 Best sellers include Edward Streeter's wartime humor, *Dere Mable*, and a Zane Grey western, *The U.P. Trail* 1918 The play *Why Marry?* by Jesse Lynch Williams wins Pulitzer Prize 1918 Willa Cather's *My Antonia* published 1918 Zionist Organization of America established

1919   The Versailles Treaty

WORLD EVENTS	POLITICS	MILITARY and FOREIGN AFFAIRS	ECONOMICS and SCIENCE	THOUGHT and CULTURE
1919 Mussolini founds Fascist party 1919-21 Civil war in Russia 1919-21 European treaties of peace signed 1920 Joan of Arc canonized 1920 First meeting of League of Nations Assembly 1921 Albert Einstein of Germany wins Nobel Prize in Physics 1921 Irish Free State proclaimed 1922 British protectorate over Egypt ended 1922 Russo-German Treaty of Rapallo 1922 Mussolini marches on Rome, seizes power 1922 Mustafa Kemal assumes Turkish dictatorship 1922 Formation of Union of Soviet Socialist	1919 Supreme Court upholds wartime sedition legislation 1919 Wilson tours country on behalf of League, suffers stroke and is bedridden 1919 "Irreconcilables" lead the League struggle against the League 1919 Volstead Act passed over presidential veto 1920 Senate refuses to ratify the League of Nations 1920 Height of "Red-scare" raids and deportations 1920 19th (women's suffrage) Amendment ratified 1920 Socialist presidential candidate Debs, in prison, polls 919,799 votes 1920 Warren G. Harding elected President 1920-33 Prohibition of domestic sale of intoxicating beverages 1921 Increased tariff on agricultural produce 1922 Fordney-McCumber Act continues 1921 trend toward higher tariffs	1919 Beginnings of agitation for a separate air arm 1919 Drafting of the Covenant of the League and Versailles Peace Treaty 1919 Wilson wins the Nobel Peace Prize 1921 Establishment of Veterans Bureau 1921 U.S. negotiates separate treaties of peace with Central Powers 1921 General Billy Mitchell conducts bombing experiments on captured German naval craft 1921-22 Washington Arms Conference produces agreement by naval powers to a limitation of capital ships 1922 U.S. creates World War Foreign Debt Commission to work out realistic schedule of payment of debts owed by the Allies to America 1922-23 Pan-American Conference proposes a regional court of justice	1919 Radio Corporation of America founded 1919 Boston police strike 1919-29 Tremendous expansion in automobile, chemical, electrical equipment, radio industries 1920 Census shows 106,466,000 inhabitants 1920 Federal Power Commission established 1920 Business recession 1920-32 Era of setbacks to organized labor 1921 Creation of Bureau of the Budget and General Accounting Offices 1921 First Immigration Quota Law passed 1921 onward Farming depression 1922 Existence of Vitamin E recognized 1922 First use of present Technicolor process 1922 Some three million homes have radios	1919 Post Office seizes and burns portions of James Joyce's *Ulysses* 1919 New York *Daily News*, first successful U.S. tabloid, founded 1919 Sherwood Anderson's *Winesburg, Ohio* published 1919 Founding of the New School for Social Research 1919-26 Jack Dempsey is world heavyweight champion 1920 Sinclair Lewis' *Main Street* published 1920 Premiere of Eugene O'Neill's play, *The Emperor Jones* 1920 F. Scott Fitzgerald's *This Side of Paradise* published 1920-27 Sacco-Vanzetti case becomes a cause célèbre 1922 Lincoln Memorial in Washington, D.C., dedicated 1922 *Reader's Digest* founded 1922 *Nanook of the North*, a pioneer documentary film, released 1922 Premiere of O'Neill's play,

1923 Frederick G. Banting of Canada shares Nobel Prize in Medicine for discovering insulin
1923 W. B. Yeats of Ireland wins Nobel Prize in Literature
1923 Unsuccessful Hitler Beer Hall Putsch in Munich
1923-30 French occupy the Ruhr districts of Germany
1923-48 British mandate in Palestine
1924 Adolf Hitler writes *Mein Kampf*
1924 Death of Lenin sets off struggle for power in U.S.S.R.
1925 Locarno treaties signed
1925-34 Hindenburg president of Germany
1926 General strike in Great Britain
1926 Germany joins the League of Nations
1926 Hirohito becomes emperor of Japan
1927 Victory of Stalinist clique in U.S.S.R.
1927 Rise to power of Chiang Kai-shek
1928 First "Five Year Plan" for Russian industrialization

1923 Death of Warren Harding; Calvin Coolidge becomes President
1923-29 Coolidge Administration, which brings "Coolidge Prosperity," marked by economy, noninterference with commerce and industry, nadir of government activity elsewhere
1924 Revelation of scandals of Harding Administration: Coolidge purges Cabinet of those implicated in Teapot Dome scandal
1924 Soldiers' Bonus Act passed over presidential veto
1924 La Follette runs for President as independent Progressive on an antitrust platform
1926-28 Revenue Acts reduce income and inheritance taxes, enable Secretary of Treasury to award extensive refunds and rebates
1927 Coolidge: "I do not choose to run for President in 1928"
1928 Naming of Al Smith as Democratic presidential candidate arouses widespread religious and cultural bigotry
1928 Hoover campaigns on platforms of "prosperity" and "rugged individualism"
1928 Herbert Hoover elected President

1923 Secretary of State Hughes urges U.S. membership in World Court
1923-24 Dawes Plan for German reparations payment
1923-35 Unsuccessful efforts to have U.S. join World Court
1924 Rogers Act reorganizes diplomatic and consular service with promotions and appointments according to merit
1924 U.S. ends its occupation of Dominican Republic
1925 U.S. sends observers to League conference on opium control, one of many similar unofficial connections with the world organization
1925 Court-martial of General Billy Mitchell for advocating an independent air arm
1926-33 U.S. intervention in Nicaragua
1927 Failure of Geneva Conference on limitation of naval armament
1927 Dwight Morrow mission to Mexico eases U.S.-Mexican tensions over oil nationalization and other issues
1928 Kellogg-Briand Pact "outlaws" war
1928 Havana Conference criticizes American interventions in Latin American affairs
1928-29 President-elect Hoover makes good-will tour of South America

1923 Robert A. Millikan wins Nobel Prize in Physics
1924 William Green succeeds Gompers as head of AFL
1925 Peak of the Florida land boom
1926 Inauguration of government aid to airlines
1927 Charles A. Lindbergh makes first solo flight from New York to Paris
1927 First vehicular underwater tunnel, in New York, opened
1927 First transmission of television signals over a considerable distance
1927-28 Drinker and Shaw invent the iron lung
1927-28 Ford replaces the Model T with the Model A
1928 Federal attempt to aid merchant marine through subsidies

1923 Height of mah-jongg craze
1924 Premiere of George Gershwin's "Rhapsody in Blue"
1924 Leopold-Loeb murder trial
1924-33 H. L. Mencken editor of *The American Mercury*
1925 Sinclair Lewis' *Arrowsmith* published
1925 Height of Charleston dance craze
1925 *The New Yorker* magazine founded
1925 Theodore Dreiser's *An American Tragedy* published
1925 Scopes trial in Dayton, Tennessee
1925 F. Scott Fitzgerald's *The Great Gatsby* published
1926 Official rules for contract bridge published
1926 Ernest Hemingway's *The Sun Also Rises* published
1926 Book-of-the-Month Club founded
1927 *The Jazz Singer* starts era of talking movies
1927 Brookings Institution chartered
1927 Babe Ruth hits 60 home runs
1927-30 Parrington's *Main Currents in American Thought* published
1928 Franz Boas' *Anthropology and Modern Life*, an attack on racial stereotype, published
1928 First Disney animated cartoon released
1928 Stephen Vincent Benet's *John Brown's Body* published

1929 The Wall Street Crash

1929 Lateran Treaty creates the Vatican City
1929 Thomas Mann of Germany wins Nobel Prize in Literature
1929 Trotsky expelled from Russia
1929-31 Gandhi civil disobedience campaign
1930 Haile Selassie becomes emperor of Ethiopia
1931 Spain becomes a republic
1931 Japanese invade Manchuria
1931 Austro-German customs union proposed
1931 Failure of *Credit Anstalt* in Vienna
1931 Statute of Westminster creates British Commonwealth
1932 Salazar becomes dictator of Portugal

1929 Federal Farm Board established
1930 Democrats win control of Congress
1930 Veterans Administration established
1930 Hoover advocates decentralized work-relief and local self-help
1931 Hawley-Smoot Tariff schedules reach all-time high
1931 Wickersham Report on Prohibition indicates local enforcement impossible, but opposes repeal
1932 Creation of Reconstruction Finance Corporation
1932 "Bonus Army" encampment in Washington dispersed
1932 Congress passes Glass-Steagall and Federal Home Loan Acts to expand credit
1932 F.D.R. pledges a "New Deal"
1932 Norris-LaGuardia Anti-Injunction Act passed

1929 Frank B. Kellogg wins the Nobel Peace Prize
1929 Young Plan revises schedule of German reparations payments
1930 U.S. officially repudiates "Roosevelt Corollary" to Monroe Doctrine
1930 London Naval Conference agrees on limitations of construction of noncapital ships
1931 Hoover proclaims one-year moratorium on Allied war-debt payments
1931 U.S. is represented at League of Nations discussion of Manchurian affairs
1932 Under Stimson Doctrine, U.S. refuses to recognize changes in territorial sovereignty achieved by breach of Kellogg-Briand Pact.

1929 Wall Street crash; beginning of the Great Depression
1929 Immigration quota system further stiffened
1929 Richard E. Byrd flight over the South Pole
1929-33 AFL membership falls from 2,934,000 to 2,127,000
1930 Census shows 123,077,000 inhabitants
1930 Planet Pluto identified
1930-36 Construction of Boulder (subsequently Hoover) Dam
1931 Urey, Murphy and Brickwedde discover heavy hydrogen isotope
1932 Wisconsin passes first unemployment insurance law in U.S.
1932 Irving Langmuir wins Nobel Prize in Chemistry
1932 Vitamin C isolated and analyzed
1932 Discovery of the positron

1929 *Middletown*, by Robert and Mary Lynd, published
1929 Thomas Wolfe's *Look Homeward Angel* published
1929 Saint Valentine's Day massacre in Chicago
1929 William Faulkner's *The Sound and the Fury* published
1930 Sinclair Lewis wins Nobel Prize in Literature
1930 First public exhibit of Grant Wood's painting, *American Gothic*
1930 Bobby Jones achieves golfing's "grand slam"
1930 Premiere of Marc Connolly's play, *The Green Pastures*
1930-35 Main period for the "proletarian novel"
1931 "Star-Spangled Banner" officially declared the U.S. national anthem
1932 Erskine Caldwell's *Tobacco Road* published
1932 Harburg and Gorney's song, "Brother, Can You Spare a Dime" epitomizes depression

FOR FURTHER READING

These books were selected for their interest and authority in the preparation of this volume, and for their usefulness to readers seeking additional information on specific points. An asterisk (*) marks works available in both hard-cover and paperback editions; a dagger (†) indicates availability only in paperback.

GENERAL READING

*Allen, Frederick Lewis, *Only Yesterday*. Harper & Row, 1931. *The Big Change*. Harper & Row, 1952.

Dulles, Foster Rhea, *America Learns to Play: A History of Popular Recreation, 1607-1940*. Peter Smith, 1952.

Durant, John, and Otto Bettmann, *Pictorial History of American Sports*. A. S. Barnes, 1952.

*Goldman, Eric F., *Rendezvous with Destiny*. Knopf, 1952.

†Hoffman, Frederick J., *The Twenties*. Collier Books, 1962.

Leighton, Isabel (ed.), *The Aspirin Age*. Simon and Schuster, 1963.

*Leuchtenburg, William E., *The Perils of Prosperity, 1914-32*. University of Chicago Press, 1958.

Link, Arthur S., and William B. Catton, *The American Epoch*. Knopf, 1963.

Morris, Lloyd R., *Postscript to Yesterday*. Random House, 1947.

Paxson, Frederic L., *Postwar Years: Normalcy, 1918-1923*. (Vol. III of American Democracy and the War Series.) University of California Press, 1948.

Soule, George, *Prosperity Decade*. Holt, Rinehart & Winston, 1947.

Sullivan, Mark, *Our Times, 1900-1925*, Vols. V and VI. Scribner's, 1933, 1935.

WAR, VICTORY AND LETDOWN (CHAPTERS 1, 2)

*Baldwin, Hanson W., *World War I: An Outline History*. Harper & Row, 1962.

Birdsall, Paul, *Versailles Twenty Years After*. Shoe String Press, 1941.

Clarkson, Grosvenor B., *Industrial America in the World War*. Houghton Mifflin, 1923.

Coit, Margaret L., *Mr. Baruch*. Houghton Mifflin, 1957.

Fredericks, Pierce G., *The Great Adventure*. E. P. Dutton, 1960.

Garraty, John A., *Henry Cabot Lodge*. Knopf, 1953.

Hagood, Johnson, *The Services of Supply*. Houghton Mifflin, 1927.

Harbord, James G., *The American Army in France, 1917-1919*. Little, Brown, 1936.

Liggett, Hunter, *A.E.F., Ten Years Ago in France*. Dodd, Mead, 1928.

Link, Arthur S., *Woodrow Wilson the Diplomatist*. Johns Hopkins Press, 1957.

*Mencken, H. L., *On Politics: A Carnival of Buncombe* (Malcolm Moos, ed.). Johns Hopkins Press, 1956.

Millis, Walter, *Road to War*. Houghton Mifflin, 1935.

Mock, James R., *Words That Won the War*. Princeton University Press, 1939.

Nicolson, Harold G., *Peacemaking, 1919*. Harcourt, Brace & World, 1939.

Palmer, Frederick, *Newton D. Baker* (2 vols.). Dodd, Mead, 1931. *Our Gallant Madness*. Doubleday, 1937.

Paxson, Frederic L., *America at War, 1917-1918*. (Vol. II of American Democracy and the World War Series.) Houghton Mifflin, 1939.

Pershing, John J., *My Experiences in the World War* (2 vols.). Frederick A. Stokes, 1931.

Rudin, Harry R., *Armistice, 1918*. Yale University Press, 1944.

Slosson, Preston W., *The Great Crusade and After, 1914-1928*. Macmillan, 1931.

Stallings, Laurence, *The Doughboys*. Harper & Row, 1963.

COMPLACENT YEARS (CHAPTER 3)

Adams, Samuel H., *Incredible Era*. Houghton Mifflin, 1939.

*Adler, Selig, *The Isolationist Impulse*. Abelard-Schuman, 1957.

†Bailey, Thomas A., *Woodrow Wilson and the Great Betrayal*. Quadrangle Books, 1963.

Freidel, Frank, *Ordeal*. (Vol. II of Franklin D. Roosevelt Series.) Little, Brown, 1954.

Johnson, Claudius O., *Borah of Idaho*. Longmans, Green, 1936.

Murray, Robert K., *Red Scare*. University of Minnesota Press, 1955.

Odegard, Peter H., *Pressure Politics: The Story of the Anti-Saloon League*. Columbia University Press, 1928.

Rae, John B., *American Automobile Manufacturers*. Chilton Co., 1959.

Schriftgiesser, Karl, *This Was Normalcy*. Little, Brown, 1948.

Sinclair, Andrew, *Prohibition, the Era of Excess*. Little, Brown, 1962.

Stein, Ralph, *The Treasury of the Automobile*. Golden Press, 1961.

Stern, Philip Van Doren, *Tin Lizzie*. Simon and Schuster, 1955.

Tumulty, Joseph P., *Woodrow Wilson As I Know Him*. Doubleday, 1921.

White, William Allen, *A Puritan in Babylon*. Macmillan, 1938.

PURSUIT OF SUCCESS (CHAPTER 4)

Allsop, Kenneth, *The Bootleggers and Their Era*. Doubleday, 1961.

Asbury, Herbert, *The Great Illusion*. Doubleday, 1950.

Harrison, Harry P., and Karl Detzer, *Culture under Canvas*. Hastings House, 1958.

Hofstadter, Richard, *Anti-Intellectualism in American Life*. Knopf, 1963.

Jensen, Oliver O., *The Revolt of American Women*. Harcourt, Brace & World, 1952.

McDonald, Forrest, *Insull*. University of Chicago Press, 1962.

Nevins, Allen, and Frank E. Hill, *Ford*, Vols. I and II. Scribner's, 1954, 1957.

Sward, Keith T., *The Legend of Henry Ford*. Holt, Rinehart & Winston, 1948.

FADS AND PORTENTS (CHAPTER 5)

Bennett, Lerone, *Before the Mayflower: A History of the Negro in America, 1619-1962*. Johnson Publishing Co., 1962.

†Busch, Francis X., *Prisoners at the Bar*. New American Library, 1962.

Danzig, Allison, and Peter Brandwein (eds.), *Sport's Golden Age*. Harper & Row, 1948.

Dulles, Foster Rhea, *Labor in America*. Thomas Y. Crowell, 1960.

Fleischer, Nathaniel S., and Sam Andre, *A Pictorial History of Boxing*. Citadel Press, 1959.

Ginger, Raymond, *Six Days or Forever?* New American Library, 1960.

Greene, Laurence, *The Era of Wonderful Nonsense*. Bobbs-Merrill, 1939.

Jacobs, Lewis, *The Rise of the American Film*. Harcourt, Brace & World, 1939.

†Manchester, William R., *Disturber of the Peace*. Collier Books, 1962.

Rice, Arnold S., *The Ku Klux Klan in American Politics*. Public Affairs Press, 1962.

Russell, Francis, *Tragedy in Dedham: The Story of the Sacco-Vanzetti Case*. McGraw-Hill, 1962.

Schorer, Mark, *Sinclair Lewis: An American Life*. McGraw-Hill, 1961.

Smith, Robert, *Baseball in America*. Holt, Rinehart & Winston, 1961.

*Stone, Irving, *Clarence Darrow for the Defense*. Doubleday, 1949.

Timberlake, James H., *Prohibition and the Progressive Movement, 1900-1920*. Harvard University Press, 1963.

Turnbull, Andrew W., *Scott Fitzgerald*. Scribner's, 1962.

*Weinberg, Arthur (ed.), *Attorney for the Damned*. Simon and Schuster, 1957.

END OF AN ILLUSION (CHAPTER 6)

Allen, Frederick Lewis, *The Lords of Creation*. Harper & Row, 1935.

*Galbraith, John K., *The Great Crash, 1929*. Houghton Mifflin, 1955.

Mitchell, Broadus, *Depression Decade, 1929-1941*. Holt, Rinehart & Winston, 1947.

Mott, Frank L., *A History of American Magazines*, Vol. IV. Harvard University Press, 1957.

Schlesinger, Arthur M. Jr., *The Crisis of the Old Order, 1919-1933*. Houghton Mifflin, 1957.

†Shannon, David A. (ed.), *The Great Depression*. Prentice-Hall, 1960.

Warren, Harris G., *Herbert Hoover and the Great Depression*. Oxford University Press, 1959.

ACKNOWLEDGMENTS

The editors of this book are particularly indebted to the following persons and institutions for their assistance in the preparation of this volume: Charles Forcey, Associate Professor of History, Rutgers University, New Brunswick, New Jersey; Frederick A. Chapman, Automobile Manufacturers Association, Detroit, Michigan; David Glick, Manager, Audio-Visual Services, and Leslie R. Henry, Curator, Department of Transportation, Henry Ford Museum, Dearborn, Michigan; James J. Bradley, Head, Automotive History Collection, Detroit Public Library, Detroit, Michigan; Henry Austin Clark Jr., Long Island Auto Museum, Southampton, New York; Edgar M. Howell, Smithsonian Institution, Washington, D.C.; John T. McCoy, New York City; Philip R. Ward, The National Archives, Washington, D.C.; Joseph H. Ewing, First U.S. Army Historian, Governors Island, New York City; Ellen E. Bantz, The Institute of Heraldry, U.S. Army, Alexandria, Virginia; William Glover and Sol Novin, Culver Pictures Inc., New York City; Roberts Jackson, Bettmann Archive, New York City; Harry B. Collins Jr., Brown Brothers, New York City; and Judy Higgins. The author, for his part, wishes to thank Alan Rau, Paul Boyer, Mrs. Frederick Burnham and Catherine Herrlich.

PICTURE CREDITS

INDEX

This symbol in front of a page number indicates a photograph or painting of the subject mentioned.

156

LIST OF MAPS FOUND IN THIS VOLUME

All maps by Rafael Palacios

PRODUCTION STAFF FOR TIME INCORPORATED

Arthur R. Murphy Jr. (Vice President and Director of Production)
Robert E. Foy, James P. Menton, Caroline Ferri and Robert E. Fraser
Text photocomposed under the direction of Albert J. Dunn and Arthur J. Dunn

XX

Printed by The Safran Printing Company, Detroit, Michigan
Bound by Rand McNally & Company, Hammond, Indiana
Paper by The Mead Corporation, Dayton, Ohio
Cover stock by The Plastic Coating Corporation, Holyoke, Massachusetts